Cen 1. — F Choudhary

Publish or Perish

Publish
or
Perish

Second edition

Edited by Philip Hills

Peter Francis Publishers

Peter Francis Publishers
The Old School House
Little Fransham
Dereham
Norfolk NR19 2JP
UK

First published 1987
Second edition 1999

A CIP catalogue record for this book
is available from the British Library

ISBN 1-870167-31-7

Printed and bound in Great Britain by Biddles Ltd,
Guildford and King's Lynn.

Contents

Notes on Contributors

Martin Askey is a lecturer and programme leader for the MSc in Environmental Management and Technology at Napier University, Edinburgh, and also works as an independent management consultant. Following MSc research while working in industry his current research activities centre on the implementation of integrated management systems for quality, environmental and health/safety issues and publishes regularly in this field. Consulting experience includes service industries such as financial advice and advertising as well as a wide range of manufacturing organisations. He is a trained auditor for both ISO9001 and ISO14001 management systems, a member of the Institute of Quality Assurance and Environmental Management, and runs a series of short courses in his specialist field.

Veronica Barnes started her career in oil and gas exploration in the North Sea. After a nine-year break bringing up two children she returned to work organising exhibitions and conferences in the United Kingdom and Europe. In 1990 she joined the Open University, first in the Department of Earth Sciences and latterly as a Course Manager in the Open University Business School. Here she managed the MBA module on Strategy and courses leading to NVQ level 4 and 5 in Management through accreditation of prior learning. She was also involved with the development of the 'Developing Women Managers' pack, used in the United Kingdom and Europe. She is currently Programme Manager for the new Law Programme at the Open University. She also enjoys running training sessions in presentation skills at the Open University.

Allison Coleman is a senior lecturer in Law at the University of Wales, Aberystwyth. She is also University Adviser on Intellectual Property and Industrial Contracts, Chairman of the University Working Party on Copyright, and Intellectual Property Law Consultant to a firm of solicitors. Allison is the author of several books, namely *The Legal Protection of Trade Secrets* (Sweet and Maxwell), *Intellectual Property Law* (Longman Law, Tax and Finance), and a co-author of *Professional Issues in Software Engineering* (UCL Press) and *Computer Law* (Blackstone); and has written numerous articles on intellectual property, and computers and the law.

Dr Mark Griffiths is a Reader in Psychology at the Nottingham Trent University. His main areas of research interest include non-drug addictions (for example, gambling, computer games, Internet, exercise, sex etc.), interactive technology (for example, computer games, Internet, virtual reality, cyberpets) and the psychology of fame. He is internationally known for his work into gambling and gaming addictions and was awarded the *John Rosecrance Research Prize* for 'Outstanding scholarly contributions to the field of gambling research' in 1994. He has published over sixty refereed research papers, numerous book chapters and over one hundred and fifty other articles. Mark also does some freelance journalism and he has appeared on over eight hundred radio and television programmes since 1988. In 1996 he was awarded a Media Fellowship by the British Association for the Advancement of Science and in 1997 was the Magnus Pike Fellow.

Nancy Harrison was educated in England, Ireland, the United States and Canada and has worked with words in a variety of contexts, in production (BBC Radio) and as an editor for a number of major publishers from Penguin to J.M. Dent. She was a member of British Standards Institute Committees concerned with the accurate use of language in the preparation of manuals and books of instruction. For some time she had a regular column called 'Watch Your Language' for the *Stag Journal* of the Society of Authors and has published several books on the use of grammar and syntax, including *Written English: A User's Manual*, as well as *Successful Writing* and *Notes on Successful Writing*, both published by Peter Francis Publishers.

James Hartley is Research Professor of Psychology at the University of Keele, Staffordshire, United Kingdom His main research interests are in written communication, with especial reference to typography and layout, and his text book *Designing Instructional Text* (Kogan Page) is now in its third edition. Professor Hartley is also well known for his research into teaching and learning in the context of higher education and his latest book in this area, *Learning and Studying: A Research Perspective* has just been published. Professor Hartley is a Fellow of the British Psychological Society and the American Psychological Association.

Dr Philip Hills is Head of the Centre for Research into Human Communication and Learning based in Cambridge. He gives workshops on publishing and research-related areas at universities across the country. He is author/editor of over seventy books and many papers in the field of education, communication skills and information technology. He is also editor of the *International Journal of Information Management* published by Elsevier Science Ltd, Oxford.

Dr Alan Ogden of the University of Leeds lectures both nationally and internationally. He was editor and curator of the British Society for the Study of Prosthetic Dentistry from 1990 to 1996. He was editor of *Guidelines in Prosthetic and Implant Dentistry* which was published in 1996 by BSSPD/Quintessence. He is scientific reviewer for a number of international and national journals, for example, *International Journal of Prosthodontics* and *Journal of Computer-Assisted Learning in Dental Education*.

Chris Rowley is currently senior lecturer in Human Resource Management and Employee Relations at City University Business School, London. He researches and publishes widely in the areas of industrial relations, human resource management, technological change, flexibility and Asia Pacific business. Amongst others things he is joint editor and reviews editor of the academic journal *Asia Pacific Business Review*, and editorial board member of *Personnel Review*. He is a frequent book and manuscript reviewer and journal article referee.

Glyn Thomas is Professor and Head of the School of Psychology at the University of Birmingham. Current research interests include the development of graphic representation in children, and of writing skills in adult writers. He has also published extensively on the psychology of learning and cognitive development.

Ann Thompson is senior lecturer in Midwifery, School of Nursing, Midwifery and Health Visiting, University of Manchester, and also has considerable clinical experience in the United Kingdom. She is the founding editor of *Midwifery*, the only international refereed journal for midwives. Her research experience is considerable and currently is interested, amongst others, in the provision of linkworker services for those from ethnic minorities and the evaluation of a maternity service for women with special needs.

Preface

ON Isaac Asimov's *Foundation and Empire* 'trilogy' at a time in the Empire's slide into destruction a hologram of Harri Seldon would appear to the people in moments of extreme crisis to advise or comment on their next step.

This second edition of *Publish or Perish* appears at a moment in academics' lives which might be considered a moment of crisis. The first edition of this book appeared some ten years ago when publication was important not only to disseminate the results of one's work but also enhance one's reputation, hence the title *Publish or Perish*. After the appearance of the first edition someone suggested that with the declining standards of research and the reportage of them, in some cases it was a question of 'publish and perish'.

Now with the pressures of the Research Assessment Exercise and the need to submit a certain numbers of papers per year to top refereed journals in order to ensure top grading for one's department, there is certainly a scramble for publication. Being the editor of one such journal the *International Journal of Information Management* I can certainly bear witness to the increased numbers of papers. As to quality it is difficult to say except that the increase in the numbers of papers received means that the journal has an increased rejection rate and therefore one might argue that this has enabled us to increase the quality of papers actually published.

The pressures to publish quality papers and report quality research are very much in the front of our minds, as is the need to scramble for the pots of grant money held out to us. Publication, track record and reputation are very important and are intertwining factors in our increasingly pressurized academic world.

Hence there is the need for this second edition of a very well received book designed to help both those setting out for the first time to penetrate the mysteries of publishing in a refereed journal and those more practised and perhaps a little cynical about the process.

There was also a need to update the book since much has changed in the intervening period, not the least being the development of the Internet, web sites, electronic journals, e-mail etc.

Rather than attempt to bring the first edition up to date it was felt necessary to start over again and this has given me the opportunity to correct some deficiencies in the original volume, to introduce new chapters and new authors.

My thanks to all of the contributors for their help and patience. Anything lacking in the present volume can be laid at my door. However, if you have any suggestions for improving this edition or if you would like a chapter considered for publication in the next, please contact me (at the address of the publishers given on the inside front page).

I hope the present volume gives you a picture not only of how to get published in refereed journals, but also conveys the essence, and the imperfections, of this process of human communication.

Philip Hills
Centre for Research into Human
Communication and Learning
Cambridge

Introduction

A new dimension has been added to the words 'publish or perish'. In the past to communicate your research results and to enhance your reputation you had to publish; lack of publication relegated you to obscurity, in effect to perish. Now, additionally, the Research Assessment Exercise is relating the future funding of your department to your publishing output in top refereed journals.

This book is about how to understand the process of getting published in refereed journals. It aims to give you not only insights into the process itself, but also to give you insights into the minds of the participants in the process. Armed with this knowledge you should be able to make more informed choices in your selection of journals, you should be able to approach editors with confidence, knowing the limitations and possibilities in the refereeing process and how to handle rejection.

It is also about the process of writing papers, in particular scientific papers, and especially writing with computers. But it ranges wider than that, as it should if you are considering building your track record, increasing your visibility on the research scene and getting grants to further your research area. To this end later chapters consider writing conference papers and writing for a number of other, non-refereed, publishing outlets.

Chapter 1 'The View from the Bridge' by Alan Ogden at the University of Leeds, himself an editor of some note, helps you to know what goes through an editor's mind when he or she considers your paper for publication. This chapter answers five key questions:

(1) Does the title and abstract give a clear indication of the contents?
(2) Does the title fit the interests of the reader?

    (3)   Have the instructions to authors been followed?

    (4)   Does the first reading impress?

    (5)   Should the paper be rejected or considered for publication?

This overview sets the scene and puts the various stages of publication in context. It includes the chain of action followed after your paper has passed the preliminary basic tests.

For a refereed journal this chain includes sending your paper to referees to get their comments, deciding whether to publish or send the paper back for revisions, or reject it. If the paper is acceptable, then it has to be slotted into a future issue with all the various stages of typesetting, proof correction and finally publication.

Referees' comments are obviously important in the context of getting your work published. Chapter 2 'The Refereeing Process' by Ann Thomson of the School of Nursing, Midwifery and Health Visiting, University of Manchester, deals with this important subject. Questions asked and answered include: Who should do it? How should a paper be refereed? How many referees? Blind or revealed? The responsibilities of a referee are considered and included is a section on what authors can expect. Both of these will help you understand what goes on while the paper is being considered and how to handle the comments you get back.

In Chapters 3 and 4 we move from a consideration of journals and the requirements of editors and referees to a consideration of the writing process.

In Chapter 3 'Writing and Computers', James Hartley of the Department of Psychology, University of Keele, looks first at the nature of writing in terms of the three stages: planning, writing and editing. The process of writing with computers for paper-based texts is then considered, followed by the differences in using computers to generate screen-based text for the World Wide Web, e-mail and other methods of electronic transmission.

Hartley also includes useful sets of guidelines including, for example, 'the characteristic strategies of productive writers' and 'guidelines for clear academic writing'. This chapter concludes with an extensive bibliography for anyone who wishes to follow up any aspect of the writing process.

Glyn Thomas, School of Psychology, University of Birmingham, contributing Chapter 4 'The Process of Writing a Scientific Paper' begins with the statement:

If you find writing difficult, you are not alone.

In this chapter you will find suggestions which are designed to help your productivity as a writer rather than just improving the style and clarity of the text. The material of this chapter is grouped into three main sections:

(1)   A theoretical background to the nature of writing itself
(2)   The practical steps in writing a paper
(3)   The methods writers use to produce text

The process of writing is discussed in terms of the classical method and the generative method which can be considered to be opposite ends of the process of writing spectrum. There is also material on writing with others, an area of increasing importance. Thomas' final conclusion is one which I thoroughly endorse:

> The initial investment of effort in reflecting on and varying your writing behaviour may well be repaid not only in better writing, but in more enjoyable writing.

Increasingly, as well as words, we need to consider visual illustrations, especially with the various forms of electronic transmission. Veronica Barnes of the Open University Business School, in Chapter 5 'Illustrations', discusses the purposes of visuals in conjunction with text and provides us with ideas on the use of different types of visuals that might be used in academic papers.

This chapter deals with photographs, paintings and drawings, maps, figures and diagrams, graphs and charts, tables and cartoons. Design of the visuals, lettering and the preparation of illustrations are all considered. The chapter ends with a checklist for good illustrations.

When we supply a disk copy of our manuscript for paper-based journals, that paper is typeset from the disk and we would expect little or no errors to occur. In practice the proofs which we are sent often contain typesetting errors and we have to correct the proofs carefully. Chapter 6 'Proof-reading and Correction' by Nancy Harrison takes us through the necessary process of correcting your proofs, and gives extracts from the BSI proof correction marks that you should use. An exercise in proof correction is given.

Chapter 7 'Copyright' is written by Allison Coleman, Department of Law, The University of Wales, Aberystwyth. This chapter first deals with the importance of copyright and the rights that copyright confers. It then considers what is protected by copyright laws, who owns copyright and how it can be assigned and licensed. Other aspects dealt with include the duration of copyright, copyright and the death of the author, and infringement of copyright. The chapter ends with a consideration of one particular exception to copyright protection – fair dealing for the purposes of research or private study which as Coleman says researchers rely heavily on as they make frequent reference to the works of others. This section explores some of the implications of this for academic writers.

The next chapter (Chapter 8) 'Living on the Front Line: stresses and strains on academic editors' by Chris Rowley, City University Business School, London, delves further into the mind of the editor and in so doing helps us to consider the realities of academic publishing in the present climate.

The contextual changes affecting, or as Rowley puts it 'afflicting' editors are grouped into 'push' and 'pull' factors, and factors increasing the volume, velocity and variability of submission. The main results and key conclusions are presented in outline.

As we mentioned at the beginning, this book is not just about getting published in refereed journals, but also about extending your activities to other writing assignments which can enhance your reputation and build your track record. The next two chapters are on this theme.

The first of these, Chapter 9, 'Writing for Refereed Journals and Conferences: the first few papers' by Martin Askey, Napier University, Edinburgh, analyses the author's experiences in building his track record over four years as an academic by writing papers for academic journals and conferences. Lessons learned are summarised under three main headings:

Journal papers
Conference papers
Publishing in general

The section on conference papers covers the choice of conference, developing an abstract, constructing the paper, attending the conference, handling questions and making contacts.

Mark Griffiths, Psychology Division, Nottingham Trent University, himself a prolific writer in a variety of publishing outlets, contributes our next chapter (Chapter 10) 'Other Publication Outlets: is there life after refereed journals?' In this chapter he shows how publishing in such outlets can benefit the academic although, as he points out, academics are sometimes reluctant to be published outside the refereed journal arena for fear of ridicule by their peers.

Griffiths does not play down the importance of peer reviewed journals but rather argues that publishing in non-refereed outlets can be done side by side with refereed academic publishing. The importance of this other publishing is that it can make our work accessible to a much wider and greater audience.

Types of outlet considered in this chapter include: writing papers for professional and vocational journals, articles and brief reports for bulletins and newsletters, letters to national newspapers, and articles for newspapers and magazines.

I supply 'The Final Word?' at the end of the book and make the prediction that whatever happens to the way we disseminate our information in years to come, via electronic or paper-based material, one thing is certain: the use of computers will immeasurably speed up and therefore bring closer our communities of writers.

Chapter 1

The View from the Bridge:
an editor's viewpoint

by Alan Ogden

WHAT goes through an editor's mind when he or she considers your paper for publication? I write from experience as an editor of a clinical and scientific journal, but much of what is said applies to journals in other academic disciplines and also to books published for the academic community. This chapter gives an overview of the process of publication; later chapters deal with the key issues at much greater length. So what processes go on in an editor's mind? Five key questions will be asked by him or her when your paper arrives.

(1) Do the title and abstract give a clear indication of the contents and are they sufficiently informative to indicate that the paper will be worth spending time considering in detail?
(2) Does the title fit in with the long-term and current interests of the journal's readership?
(3) Has the author followed the instructions to contributors ?
(4) Does a first reading impress?
(5) Should we reject the paper outright or consider it for publication?

This chapter will attempt to explore and answer each one of them.

Importance of Title and Abstract

You should pay particular attention to the title and abstract as these will actually be read by many more people than the paper itself and, if set out clearly, will encourage readers to seek out the full version. Since the abstract may also be published separately by secondary journals, the contents should be self-sufficient and not rely on the reader being able to see the whole paper.

The abstract may well be the first thing you commit to paper when you start, but do not hesitate to modify, or even re-write it, if the emphasis of your paper changes as you develop your own understanding of what you are reporting.

Expectations of the Journal and Readership

Before submitting a paper, and preferably before starting to write, it is import-ant to think carefully about the correct form and place for its publication and to identify the community you are trying to reach. You need to be sure in your mind of the answers to a number of questions which will help you to clarify what you are trying to say.

- Is the work complete or are you making a preliminary announce-ment?
- Should there be more than one paper, possibly in different journals, to bring different aspects of the work to the attention of different groups of readers?
- Would a short note or a letter to the editor be sufficient and perhaps more likely to be read by a large number of people?

It is always a good idea to discuss the possibilities with an experienced academic. Severe self-criticism at this stage may save you from painful and public criticism by others.

Your paper must be original work by yourself and your co-authors, and should not have been published before. Publishing the same paper or results twice, especially if the first publication is not referred to, can damage an author's reputation. Over-publication can lead to further complications such as copyright infringement. Originality is not, however, invalidated by a pre-liminary communication provided that in the full paper much more detail is given and the preliminary communication is properly referred to and referenc-ed. On rare occasions duplicate publication may be allowed if the paper is addressed to very different audiences or in a different language or country, but only with the *full knowledge* and *consent* of all the editors involved.

You will also need to decide on authorship including those (and only those) who contributed substantially to the work. All those named as authors must, of course, see and approve at least the final draft; they may all be required later to sign a form allocating copyright to the publisher. Establish too the order in which the authors will be listed – sometimes the journal may have a policy on this but usually it is left to the authors – and which author should be named for correspondence related to the paper after publication.

Selection of the appropriate journal to which to submit the paper is a crucial decision. Do this *before* writing the paper, so that the detailed style of the journal and, in particular, any "Instructions to Authors" that it has produced, can be borne in mind while writing the paper. It is useful to take time in choosing a relevant journal. Look at recent issues of any publications you are considering to ensure that papers in the same general field as your own are regularly being published in it. This will help to indicate whether your paper will reach the target audience through that journal and also whether the journal will regard your paper as suitable for its readership.

You should aim for a prestigious journal from which papers are frequently cited by others. Look at the delay time between the receipt or acceptance of a paper (normally printed at the end of a paper) and the *actual* publication date. Consider whether the journal can reproduce properly any illustrative material that you need. Publishers are naturally reluctant to include large numbers of illustrations, particularly if these are of a kind that is expensive to reproduce, such as colour plates or large illustrations requiring a fold-out from the normal page size or a separately printed sheet in a folder at the end of the journal, and only certain journals will even contemplate the inclusion of such material. Even these journals will try to limit such material to what is really essential, so authors should think very carefully whether their work could not be presented without these complications. However, if the illustrations are essential, this may dictate your choice of journal.

When you have decided on the journal, obtain and use its "Instructions to Authors" which are published on or inside the covers of the journal, or as a separate brochure referred to in the journal and obtainable from the editor. Spend time studying these instructions: it can save a great deal of unnecessary and tedious re-writing when the paper should otherwise have been finished.

Instructions to Contributors

The typed version *must* meet the requirements of the journal or it may be rejected out of hand.

Presentation, Layout, Spacing, Pagination, Footnotes

Usually this means typing on one side of the paper only, with double spacing and wide margins. This is for a very real reason. Editing, even of a well-prepared paper, involves writing many comments and instructions on the typed sheet, and, if there is insufficient room, irritation and confusion can set in both with reviewers and the printer because the instructions are hard to interpret.

Word-processors are now essential in typing papers because of their ability to make suggested corrections *without* introducing further errors, and all good-quality word-processors with output from laser printers or good quality inkjets can produce excellent typescripts.

Number of Copies

Clear instructions will be given as to how many originals and how many copies are to be sent. Editors are not impressed if even simple instructions are ignored and journal staff have to do additional photocopying. Is a copy of the document also required on disk, and, if so, in what format? Do they require simple ASCII text files or a formatted document in a named version of a word-processing program? If you are not clear what the requirements mean, seek early advice from a computer-literate colleague rather than risk wasting your precious time.

Units of Measure

Style rules (capitalization, italicization, spacing etc.) for metric units are now well established and should be adhered to as evidence of the professionalism of the authors. Most journals are now moving towards SI units (Système International d'Unités), but it is by no means universal, particularly in the United States. Instructions to authors need to be consulted on these issues.

References

Do ensure that your list of references is in the specified form and contains the correct amount of detail for your chosen journal. Instructions for authors usually state *very precisely* how references to papers in journals and sections in books should be presented and listed. This may seem pedantic but could well be grounds for immediate rejection if you have not bothered to follow these instructions. Ensure that all your references appear in the reference list and that every reference is actually quoted in the text. Such elementary mistakes are easily spotted by referees and will prejudice them against your paper.

Most scientific journals specify that references are arranged in the order in which they are first cited in the text. Name and date citations in the text are replaced by a number, often in superscript. The name and date or Harvard system is widely used in non-scientific journals, listing references in the alphabetical order determined by the family name of the first author. Most European names are easily arranged in the correct order, but uncertainties can arise with definite articles or particles, such as 'van' or 'de' preceding the family name, with compound family names (as in Spain) or with middle-eastern or oriental names.

Figures and Tables

Figures and tables should be referred to and numbered (roman or arabic) in the preferred style of the journal. Diagrams should be supplied in the form requested by the publication, properly drawn on separate drawing film or special paper, or computer-produced and printed with high definition (300 dpi minimum). Diagrams and illustrations should preferably be larger than the published version will be, as photo-reduction will sharpen them up and minor imperfections will be smoothed out. Photographs should also be supplied in the specific form and dimensions requested by the publication.

Copyright

Permission has to be obtained to use any material for which the copyright belongs to others, particularly illustrations or tables. Authors are often very cavalier about copyright but publishers are extremely anxious to avoid any chance of litigation or allegations of infringement of copyright.

First Impressions

An editor looks for a paper that is written clearly and concisely, with a well-thought out structure indicated by appropriate headings. Are the authors' conclusions justified or are they based on a tottering edifice of wishful thinking?

It is always good practice to write for the understanding of someone for whom English is a second language. Two short sentences are always better than a long rambling one with multiple qualifying phrases. Break large paragraphs up into smaller units to help the reader navigate quickly through the paper, without losing his or her place and keeping a sense of direction. Avoid metaphors and highly idiomatic expressions, technical jargon or slang and unnecessary synonyms. After using your word-processor's spell-checker enhanced to cope with your specialist vocabulary, read a printout of your paper very carefully and thoroughly to check for typing errors or omissions. However by this stage you will have lost the ability to 'see' your paper and your eyes will read what your brain expects to be there. It is therefore essential to ask someone other than one of the authors to read it through, to spot errors in syntax and typing. Meanings that are self-evident to the authors may not be so to others. (This chapter has itself gone through this process and ambiguities in the preliminary draft have been detected and, I hope, eliminated.)

Statistical techniques are becoming increasingly complex, with ever higher standards and it is always worth seeking specialist statistical advice at an early stage, before you process your data. Your conclusions must be defensible against statistical attack. You do not want to have to re-process all the data months after submission because your paper has been rejected on statistical grounds.

Rejection or Acceptance – what next?

If you have prepared properly as suggested above, your submission will successfully pass the preliminary basic tests. Now that it is to be seriously considered, the editor will then start the following actions.

Send to Referees for Judgement and Comments

Copies of your paper will be sent to referees selected by the editor because of their specialist knowledge, professional standing and good judgement. They will review your paper and prepare a confidential report for the editor. If heavily reliant on statistics, your paper may also be passed on for a specialist opinion on that aspect of your work. As good referees are bound to be busy and sought-after, weeks or even months may go by before they produce their reports. It is important for authors not to be too impatient. High quality referees will need adequate time to consider your paper properly before making a judgement.

When their replies have been received, the editor, perhaps in discussion with an editorial committee, will decide whether, in the light of the referees' comments, your paper will be accepted as it stands, accepted only after modification, or rejected. It is not uncommon for the referees to differ, especially over style, and the editor's decision is final.

Editor's Decisions

The editor then has to decide

(a)   to accept the paper for publication with minor amendments, or
(b)   to return the paper to the authors for re-submission after suggested amendments, or
(c)   to decline publication with a letter indicating reasons and perhaps advising future action.

It is rare for a paper to be accepted without any changes. If these are minor, even if there are many, the editor will ask for the authors' agreement to a list of the proposed changes.

You will often be sent an anonymous copy of the referees' comments, and even if the recommendation is acceptance, you may be asked if you wish to make changes in the light of the comments made. You should always take the referees' comments seriously. Even though you have worked long and hard to perfect your paper, you should swallow your pride and recognize that if these referees, chosen by the editor as experts in your field, feel that the paper needs to be changed, you should try to meet their requests.

If the journal rejects your paper, you should not abandon it unless the referees have drawn attention to major flaws in the work. This is particularly true if you have sent it to a prestigious journal – some disciplines have very high rejection rates in such journals. Lock (1985) reported, for example, that the *British Medical Journal* rejected 79 per cent of the papers submitted to it in the study period, but that 73 per cent of these (that is, 58 per cent of the originally submitted papers) were subsequently published elsewhere. Thus a paper, modified to deal with any substantial criticism from the referees, should either be sent back to the original publication or sent to a more appropriate journal.

Publication Dates?

The editor will have provisional plans for future editions and may be able to give you some idea of when your work will be published.

Reprints Required

Think about this well in advance. Journals differ in their approach to reprints. Some offer a certain number free of charge, others insist on payment, which may be astonishingly expensive if colour plates are involved. However all journals insist that whatever the authors require must be ordered *before* publication. Once the print run has been completed it is impossible or very expensive to produce reprints.

Approved Copy to Printer

Assuming that your paper has now been accepted by a journal, the editor or copy-editor will go through marking any stylistic changes required to bring the paper into line with the journal's house style, or correcting any obvious errors of spelling or grammar, and marking for the typesetter any unusual or ambiguous letters or symbols. The article will then be set up in print and proofs sent to the editor and then the author.

Proofs

In the past this was often a 'galley proof' which had not been put into individual pages, but with the advent of computer typesetting it has become more common to go straight to a paged proof. This will be examined and further corrected, if necessary, by the editor or one of his or her staff.

When the proof is received the author should read it carefully, particularly noting whether any changes made by the editor have altered the sense from what is intended. Unless this is so, stylistic changes should be accepted, but changes that have led to inaccuracies should be corrected, as should any typesetting errors, using the standard proof-correcting marks[1] because these are unambiguous.

This is not the stage at which to introduce new ideas or to revise the paper. By this stage a tight schedule to publication is probably involved so the proofs should be returned promptly by a deadline. Corrections received after this may well be ignored anyway, as the editor will probably already have sent his or her amendments back to the typesetter.

Once the editor has incorporated his or her own and the authors'

---

[1]   British Standard BS 5261: PART 2 1976 (1991) Copy preparation and proof correction – specification of typographic requirements, marks for copy preparation and proof correction, proofing procedure. British Standards Institution, London.

corrections, the typesetter will produce a final proof to check that the correct-ions have been correctly made (this is not normally sent to authors) and the article is sent with the rest of the issue to the printers and binders.

Publication

If all goes well your masterpiece will at last appear in print as a truly professional piece of work, reflecting well both on you and the publisher. But remember that it is only as a result of attention to detail at every stage that there has been a successful outcome.

With the increasing pressures on all academics, by the time your paper appears you will almost have forgotten it, having moved on in your interests, and you will probably already be enmeshed in the process of producing further papers.

Resulting Correspondence

Your publication may well generate discussion or even controversy amongst the readership and this will usually be addressed in the first instance to the editor. He or she will give you the right to reply but will impose a strict deadline so that the correspondence can be published whilst of immediate interest to the readership. Even if such criticisms are ill-informed they can take a great deal of time to deal with. An effective system of review by the journal should mean that you have little to fear. In fact it is depressing if your work excites no active response at all from the readership.

Longer-term correspondence is usually sent to the named author. Apart from dozens of cards requesting reprints, even in this age of photocopying, these contacts may well lead to long term co-operation or rivalry, both of which encourage future work.

Finally

This overview has set the scene and put the various stages of publication in their wider context. The following chapters will explore some of the issues raised in this chapter. I hope it has whetted your appetite. Come on in – the water's warmer than you think!

References

Booth, V. (1985) *Communicating in Science: Writing and Speaking.* Cambridge: Cambridge University Press.

Farr, A.D. (1985) *Science Writing for Beginners.* Oxford: Blackwell Scientific Publications.

Huth, E.J. (1990) *How to Write and Publish Papers in the Medical Sciences.* Philadelphia: ISI Press.

Legat, M. (1991) *An Author's Guide to Publishing.* London: Robert Hale.

Lock S. (1985) *A Difficult Balance: editorial peer review in medicine.* London: Nuffield Provincial Hospitals Trust.

O'Connor, M. and Woodford, F.P. (1975) *Writing Scientific Papers in English.* Amsterdam: Associated Scientific Publishers.

other reasons peculiar to any given journal. Moreover, when peer review did come, it was institutionalized in a variety of ways. (1327)

However, evaluation of the process has only a relatively recent history and there is a need for this to continue (see Bailar and Patterson, 1985; Rennie, 1993; Rennie and Flanagin, 1994; Smith, 1994; 1997).

Who should Referee?

Most journals adopt a policy of the editor selecting those who should referee papers (Lock, 1985), and in order to do that he or she has to be an expert in that particular field. With increasing specialism in scientific and medical practice this may be increasingly difficult and authors may be right in asking 'Who is my peer?' However, more recently editors have invited referees to nominate themselves (Gouldbeck-Wood, 1998), and now the process has moved even further on with the result that when submitting a manuscript authors are invited to nominate the most appropriate referees (Tonks, 1995). The rationale for the latter is that new researchers in a field will be the most aware of those with the expertise to assess the value of their work. Whilst this would seem a logical progression it has the somewhat dangerous potential for authors to nominate those who, they think, will give a favourable view! There is also the problem that because the nominated referee is aware of the work of the author he or she may not be objective in considering a manuscript.

How should a Paper be Refereed?

Views on how this should be managed vary. Lock (1985: 16) reproduces the Royal Society's guidelines for peer review that 'every paper submitted to the journal for publication should be refereed'. However, journals such as the *British Medical Journal*, the *Journal of the American Medical Association* and *The Lancet* operate a 'triage' policy of considering all manuscripts by in-house editors to assess whether a manuscript should be sent to be refereed (Lock, 1985; Sharp, 1990; Lundberg and Williams, 1991). They do this because of the large number of manuscripts received in comparison to the amount of potential publishing space (Lock, 1985; Sharp, 1990). It is obvious that both practices have disadvantages. If all manuscripts received are sent to be refereed then the referees are in danger of receiving manuscripts on topics not suitable for that journal or of such poor standard that they have no chance of being published. My experience has led me to the conclusion that a happy medium has to be struck. Prior to a paper being sent to referees there should be some in-house assessment of the paper to see first whether it comes within the aims and scope of the journal and second, whether the paper appears to reach the academic standard required for publication in the journal. In reviewing the literature I have not come across any reports of how this first level of assessment is undertaken. When a paper having fulfilled the aims and scope of the journal is submitted to me I read the abstract, and in particular read the methods section of the paper. Provided that the abstract is sufficiently clear, – the 'Structured Abstract' format (Haynes *et al.*, 1990) is used –, so that I can understand the content of the paper and the methods are adequately described so that I could replicate the study if I so wished, I then send the paper to be refereed. Whilst it is possible that bias in the rejection process can be introduced at this stage it is also unacceptable to give referees, who are usually busy people over-burdened with work (Judson, 1994), the trouble of reading a paper, which has no chance of being published, or an occasional crank paper (Bailar and Patterson, 1985).

Bailar and Patterson report 'considerable vagueness in the expectations of editors and the instructions provided to reviewers' (655). In suggesting a checklist for the writing of a review, Oxman (1994) states that passengers in an aeroplane are grateful that a pilot has a list of points to check before take off. If there was no check list it would be possible for vital safety points to be inadvertently omitted. He suggests that whilst 'faulty reviews may not seem as perilous as faulty airplanes' it is better to ensure that all points are addressed rather than leave this to chance since, if practitioners are going to use reviews to 'guide decisions about health care, misleading reviews can indeed be deadly'. However, Sharp (1990) states that despite having no check list referees for *The Lancet* appear to make comments on all the points they wish to be addressed. I have been asked to referee papers by completing a blank sheet of paper and have not been sure what to comment on. I have also had referees' reports of some of my own papers where it is obvious that the referee has had no information on what the editor wants to know about the paper. In the latter case I have found the reports singularly unhelpful and the referees have had a tendency to comment on issues irrelevant to the publication of the manuscript. Lundberg and Williams (1991) report that in the editorial and peer review process at the *Journal of the American Medical Association* they ask:

- Is the material original?
- Are the data valid?
- Are the conclusions reasonable and justified by the data?

- Is the information important?
- Is the article of general medical interest?
- Is the writing clear or can it be made clear?

The check list used in my journal, reproduced in Figure 2.1 below, is similar to that used at the *Journal of the American Medical Association*, and, as can be seen, asks the referee specific questions about the scientific merit of the paper. The section asking for further information allows the referee to expand on the points in the check list. Comments in this section should always be objective and constructive (Ingelfinger, 1974). There is conflicting opinion on whether referees should be asked to recommend a paper for publication. The Royal Society guidelines state that a definite recommendation should be given (Lock, 1985) but Relman and Angell (1989) state that reviewers are consultants to editors and not decision-makers.

There is plenty of evidence of inadequate presentation of statistical information with ensuing eronious results (Lock, 1985; Pocock *et al.*, 1987; Gore *et al.*, 1992). A policy has now been adopted by *The Lancet* that all papers containing statistics are to be sent to statistical referees after the initial refereeing process, and Gardner *et al.* (1986) have published the check list used at the *British Medical Journal* to assess the statistical content of a paper. To speed up the refereeing process in my quarterly journal the statistical referee is included in the initial refereeing process where appropriate.

Referees' Responsibilities

Referees must recognise limitations in their abilities and should not attempt to referee a paper on a topic outside their area of expertise. Also, if they cannot complete the report within the time required by the journal editor the paper must be returned immediately with an explanation of why they cannot consider the paper on this occasion. Finally, referees must treat the contents of the paper as confidential and should not share the contents with anyone else. There are many examples of material in papers submitted for potential publication being made available before that paper was published and of material in a submitted paper being stolen (Lock, 1985). An editor would not have sent a paper to a referee if the topic was not of interest to the referee and there may be occasions when the contents are of particular interest. However, it is unethical to reveal the contents of the paper before publication.

		YES	NO

1. Is the topic within the scope of MIDWIFERY? ____ ____

2. Is the subject matter of the article of sufficient importance to merit publication? ____ ____

3. Does the article contain original material? ____ ____

4. Is adequate reference made to previous work on the subject? ____ ____

5. If a research report:

    (I)   Are the design and methods adequately described? ____ ____

    (ii)   Are there defects in the design and methods of the work which may have led to erroneous conclusions? ____ ____

    (iii)   Are the results presented adequately? ____ ____

6. Are all the figures, tables and other illustrations clearly labelled, and are they all necessary? ____ ____

7. Is the discussion relevant and concise? ____ ____

8. Does the language or presentation need attention before publication? ____ ____

CONFIDENTIAL COMMENTS TO THE EDITOR

Please comment here on your decisions above and any other aspects you consider relevant.

Figure 2.1: Peer review assessment form for *Midwifery* (reproduced by kind permission of Harcourt Brace, publishers of *Midwifery*)

The referee has to read the paper, according to a required check list, where one exists, or to a personal list where one does not exist. This procedure is time-consuming if it is to be undertaken thoroughly and with the same care and consideration that the author will have used in writing the paper. Referees have a responsibility to check the references used in the supporting literature, the methods and discussion. Where the referee is an expert in the area this will not be an onerous task as most of the literature will be known. However, the referee should be particularly vigilant to spot the use of secondary sources. These are someone else's interpretation of someone else's work. For example, I found when I was conducting a review of the literature on the position a woman should adopt in the second stage of labour that Moore (1983), and others, quoted Bonica (1967). On reading Bonica I found that he was quoting the work of Mengert and Murphy (1933) who had conducted their research on non-pregnant women and had specifically cautioned against extrapolating their work to the second stage of labour.

Whilst it is not easy to detect, referees should be alive to the problem of multiple publishing of one piece of research. Waldron (1992) undertook a Medline search of bibliographic details and abstracts of the papers cited by all authors published in the British Journal of Industrial Medicine in the years 1988-90. He found that 6 per cent of the articles published in 1988 had been published elsewhere, in 1989 it was 8 per cent and in 1990 12 per cent, suggesting a significant increase over time. Since few of the articles were reproduced in their entirety in another journal and the findings were frequently published with modifications, it was difficult for referees to spot. The listings of the authors were also altered according to the speciality of the journal so that 'if an epidemiologist and a radiologist were the authors, the epidemiologist would appear first for the epidemiological journal and the radiologist for the radiological journal' (1029).

How Many Referees?

The number of referees used to consider an article varies from journal to journal and on how the editorial process is managed. Lock (1985) reports that the *British Medical Journal* used only one referee because, statistically, most articles were likely to be rejected and any considered suitable by a referee were then considered by the five medically qualified members of the 'hanging committee'. However, Lock (1985) also reveals that at *Current Anthropology* a paper would be sent to at least fifteen referees. In reporting various factors about the *Journal of the American Medical Association* Lundberg and

Williams (1991) state that the number of reviewers used per manuscript in 1990 ranged from 'one to more than five'. Manuscripts accepted for publication had a mean of 2.78 reviewers whilst those which were rejected had a mean of 2.86. There are journals which use only a single referee. I know of two in the nursing profession, and it is generally considered that using only one referee is not as rigorous as using two or more. The number used will depend on the discipline and Lock (1985) suggests that it is usual for two external referees to be consulted. The peer review guidelines of *The Royal Society* state that no paper should be rejected on the adverse report of one referee.

Blind or Revealed?

There is much debate about whether authors and referees should know the identity of each other. Whilst some journals have operated a 'single blind' policy whereby referees know who the authors are but the authors do not know the identity of the referees, more recently a policy of a double-blind process has been adopted so that, in theory at least, the referees do not know the identity of authors. Double-blind refereeing has been shown to provide more unbiased reviews (Fisher *et al.*, 1994; Ong and Abbott, 1994) and the quality of the reviews is of a higher standard (McNutt *et al.*, 1990). It is not always easy to 'blind' a paper because an author has only to refer to his or her own previous work in the area for at least the 'stable' where the research was undertaken to become obvious, if not the actual authors. McNutt *et al.* (1990) reported that in their randomised controlled trial of blinding 27 per cent of the referees were aware of the authors' identity. I have had referees return papers to me when they recognise the identity of the paper's authors, despite our practice of 'blinding' the papers, and ask that the paper be reviewed by someone else. It would seem fair to all parties that either a refereeing system should be double blind or revealed. It would seem to be singularly unfair, for example, for the referee to know the identity of the author, but for the author not to know the identity of the referee and *vice versa.*

The Advantages

Peer review effectively screens unsatisfactory manuscripts (Abby *et al.*, 1994), it improves the quality of papers (Rennie and Flanagin, 1994, Scott and Smith, 1996; Weller, 1996) and improves the ultimate quality of research (Relman and Angell, 1989). Sharp (1990) suggests that peer review provides the opportunity to remove bias and Roberts *et al.* (1994) report that the readability of the paper is improved. Secondary review of papers submitted to the *Journal of Pediatrics* suggested that peer review was reliable in that 80 per cent of previously accepted papers were recommended for publication and the others, whilst not considered to be of high priority, were not recommended for rejection (Garfunkel *et al.*, 1990).

The Disadvantages

Peer review has many critics but it has to be remembered that it is a social process, not a scientific one (Relman and Angell, 1989; Kroll, 1990). It is time-consuming, expensive, delays the publication of new knowledge (Lock, 1985) and only allows conventional (Knoll, 1990) or conservative (Redfern, 1994) research to be published.

One of the major disadvantages of peer review is that it cannot prevent or always detect fraud, or piracy (Relman and Angell, 1989; Rennie, 1993). In discussing this Lock (1985) suggests that one of the most famous cases is that of Sir Cyril Burt who fooled educationalists, and the public, about the relationship between intelligence and inheritance. Lock (1985) states that the medical equivalent was a cardiovascular researcher, John Darsee, who amongst other things invented data and co-authors. The major problem is that anyone determined to get something published will get it published somewhere, no matter how trivial the contents of the paper and how obscure the journal. Rennie and Flanagin (1994: 91) state that 'editors should assist in or encourage research to establish baseline data on the prevalence of scientific fraud'. Editors of British medical journals and medical societies are so concerned about the current potential for fraud that they have called for the establishment of a national body to investigate allegations of misconduct and fraud (Williams, 1998).

It is also difficult for peer review to detect cases of plagiarism (Lock, 1985; Marshall, 1998). Writers have been able to build up considerable portfolios of articles which they have not written entirely themselves.

In complaining about the absence of research on the reproducibility of peer review Ernst *et al.* (1993: 296) sent a paper which had been submitted to a journal to 45 'experts'. As a result of this they report extreme judgements from 'unacceptable' to 'excellent' on the nine quality criteria used by the journal. They suggest that the reproducibility was disappointingly low and that the absence of reliability suggested 'seems unacceptable for anyone aspiring to publish in peer reviewed journals'. However, Wolff (1993) comments that Ernst *et al.* had a poor response rate (69 per cent), presented their data inadequately and that for only two of the nine criteria did all the respondents give an opinion. Despite the methodological problems Wolff suggests that three quarters of the sample considered the paper worth publishing with modifications. Relman and Angell (1989) suggest that defects in the editorial process are not due to the process itself but to inadequate editorial supervision of the process.

Results of Refereeing on Publication

Chalmers (1990) suggests that the findings only get to be published if they are positive outcomes, studies reporting negative findings appear to be rejected and he suggests that editors should mend their ways and publish both negative and positive findings. However, Dickersin *et al.* (1992) showed that the bias does not exist at the editorial level but at the investigator level in that investigators did not submit for publication any manuscript reporting negative findings.

What can Authors Expect

If the paper is to be subjected to the refereeing process the author can expect to be told how long the refereeing process should take. Delays in the reviewing process are considered by authors to be very irksome (Sweitzer and Cullen, 1994). If that period is going to be exceeded then the author can expect the editor to inform them of that fact and of the reason for the delay. The editor of an international journal uses referees from all round the world and whilst electronic mail does considerably speed the process of sending material abroad, not all referees, particularly those in developing countries, have access to this method of communication. The editor and referee are then subject to the vagaries of the postal system.

The author can expect a courteous letter stating what the decision of the process is and, unless the paper is accepted without change, a rare phenomenon, an enclosed statement of the referees' comments. I do not usually send copies of the referees' comments, first, because there are occasions when referees disagree, and it is singularly unhelpful to an author to receive conflicting reports (Sweitzer and Cullen, 1994; Weller, 1996); and then the referees may have made comments which conflict with either the editorial or publishing policy. It is my practice to write a report combining the comments of the referees and including any comments/queries that I may have as editor. This practice means that frequently authors receive up to 30 points which need consideration. The covering letter that I send will indicate whether I expect the author to revise the manuscript.

Having received a letter informing them that the paper is not ready for publication authors should not immediately 'go into a decline' or commit suicide. The letter and manuscript should be put away in a drawer for at least 48 hours. The authors should then arrange for some quiet time and obtain whatever liquid they use as a restorative. They should then go through the points of the referees' comments very slowly and re-read the manuscript in the light of the comments. During this re-reading they should decide whether the referees' comments are reasonable. If they are, and provided the research is not flawed, they should be able to revise the manuscript so that it reaches a publishable standard. If they do not agree with the comments then it is perfectly acceptable to inform the editor of this disagreement and the reason for it. The editor will enter into a dialogue with the authors until either the disagreement is resolved or an agreement reached that the paper will not be published in that journal.

It is my experience that if the author revises the paper according to the instructions then acceptance for publication will ensue. Dewey (1993) and Bhopal and Parkin (1993) report experiences of returning their manuscripts according to referees' comments only to receive further requests for different revisions. Whilst I accept that there are occasions when further queries are raised because of elucidations in the revised manuscript, a situation should never arise where further points which existed in the original manuscript need to be raised. The revised manuscript should only be referred to the original referees if the editor is not confident that the authors have dealt with the points adequately. If this occurs then the original referees should be sent a copy of their comments, a copy of the comments sent to the author and any response from the authors to the comments, as well as a copy of the revised manuscript. It is not my practice to send a revised manuscript out to different referees. This has happened to colleagues and only leads to confusion and should be unnecessary if the original refereeing process is robust.

If the paper does have to be returned to referees the authors should be informed of this and told when they should know the outcome of the process. If the paper does not have to go back to the referees the editor should inform the author whether the paper has been accepted or not, and, if yes, that they will receive the proofs in due course.

Garfunkel *et al.* (1990) and Sweitzer and Cullen (1994) undertook surveys of authors' views of the peer review process at the Journal of Pediatrics and the *Journal of Clinical Anaesthesia* respectively. Unsurprisingly the response rate from those whose papers were rejected was lower (67 per cent in the

Journal of Pediatrics and 43 per cent in the *Journal of Clinical Anaesthesia)* than for those whose paper was accepted (90 per cent in the *Journal of Pediatrics* and 67 per cent in the *Journal of Clinical Anaesthesia).* The editors' communications in the Journal of Pediatrics were evaluated more positively by those whose paper had been accepted than by those whose paper had been rejected but there was no difference in the evaluation of the referees' reports (Garfunkel *et al.,* 1990). Two thirds of authors whose papers were rejected, but were invited to re-submit, by the *Journal of Clinical Anaesthesia* reported that the review process had improved the quality of the papers (Sweitzer and Cullen, 1994).

Sweitzer and Cullen (1994) suggest that in order to improve the peer review process the views of authors should be taken into consideration. Dewey (1993) states that too often authors are maltreated by editors, and Bhopal and Parkin (1993) describe their experience as 'torture'. When authors state that the experience 'swept away their confidence in the peer review process' (717) it seems to be particularly important to review the process, since authors, as well as readers, and those who are the recipients of our professional expertise (students, clients, patients) are the consumers of refereed journals.

Does Refereeing Have a Future?

Judson (1994) suggests that at the beginning of the twenty-first century, whilst some form of assessment of manuscripts will still exist, it will be radically different from the procedures followed today. He suggests that it will be an open process where researchers will critique each others' work in a 'more thoroughly responsible and accountable manner (Judson, 1994: 94). This would fit with Scott and Smith's (1996) suggestion that referees should have authorship with authors in order that they should become more accountable. Judson states that if the peer review process is more open it will be less 'capricious, rigid and subject to abuse'. Rennie and Flanagin (1994) suggest that there is a need to adopt more uniform standards of peer review.

Colaianni (1994) suggests that if a journal is refereed then there should be a very clear statement in the journal of how the process is undertaken which would go some way to demystifying the process. I realise that, whilst it is stated in the "Instructions to Authors of Midwifery" that the journal is refereed blind, that is all that is said about the process, and I will be taking steps to remedy this. I will also be adopting the policy recommended by Scott and Smith (1996) of providing formal feedback to all referees of the result of the assessment of all papers they have reviewed. Schulman *et al.* (1994)

recommend training for reviewers. This may be more difficult to achieve by a journal with relatively few resources, but if the best quality material is to be published then it is important that the best advice is received by editors. New reviewers have indicated to me that being required to complete the assessment form (Figure 2.1) sharpens their critical reading. Perhaps this is one way of providing training.

Relman and Angell (1989: 829) state that 'Peer review has its limitations, but it is hard to imagine how we could get along without it'. Despite his bad experiences Dewey (1993: 320) reports that 'many of my papers have been improved substantially as a result of the feedback I have received'. Perhaps if editors were to supervise the process more assiduously, as recommended by Relman and Angell (1989), readers, authors and the recipients of the professional expertise of those reading the journals would be more satisfied with the results.

References

Abby, M., Massey, M.D. and Galandiuk, S. (1994) "Peer review is an effective screening process to evaluate medical manuscripts", *Journal of the American Medical Association*, 272 (2): 105-7.

Bailar, J.C., Patterson, K. (1985) "Journal peer review, the need for a research agenda", *New England Journal of Medicine*, 321 (10): 654-7.

Bhopal, R.S., Parkin, D.W. (1993) "Authors have rights too", *British Medical Journal*, 306: 716-7.

Burnham, J.C. (1990) "The evolution of peer review", *Journal of the American Medical Association*, 263 (10):1323-9.

Chalmers, I. (1990) "Underreporting research is scientific misconduct", *Journal of the American Medical Association*, 263 (10): 1405-8.

Colaianni, L.A. (1994) "Peer review in journals", indexed in *Index Medicus. Journal of the American Medical Association*, 272 (2): 156-8.

Dickersin, K., Min, Yuan-I, Meinert, C.L. (1992) "Factors influencing publication of research results", *Journal of the American Medical Association*, 267 (3): 374-8.

Dewey, M. (1993) "Authors have rights too", *British Medical Journal*, 306: 318-20.

Ernst, E., Saradeth, T. and Resch, K.L. (1993) "Drawbacks of peer review, *Nature*, 363: 296.

Fisher, M., Friedman, S.B. and Strauss, B. (1994) "The effects of blinding on acceptance of research papers by peer review", *Journal of American Medical Association*, 272 (2): 143-6.

Gardner, M.J., Machin, D. and Campbell, M.J. (1986) "Use of check lists in assessing the statistical content of medical studies", *British Medical Journal*, 292: 810-2.

Garfunkel, J.M., Lawson, E.E., and Hamrick, H.J. (1990) "Effect of acceptance or rejection on the author's evaluation of peer review of medical manuscripts", *Journal of the American Medical Association*, 263 (19): 1376-8.

Goldbeck-Wood, S. (1998) "What makes a good reviewer of manuscripts? The BMJ invites you to join its peer review process", *British Medical Journal*, 316.

Gore, S.M., Jones, G. and Thompson, S.G. (1992) "*The Lancet's* statistical review process: areas for improvement by authors", *The Lancet*, 340: 100-2.

Haynes, R.B., Mulrow, C.D. and Huth, E.J. (1990) "More informative abstracts revisited: a progress report", *Annals of Internal Medicine*, 113: 69-76.

Ingelfinger, F.J. (1974) "Peer review in biomedical publication", *The American Journal of Medicine*, 56: 686-92.

Judson, H.F. (1994) "Structural transformations of the sciences and the end of peer review", *Journal of the American Medical Association*, 272 (2): 92-4.

Knoll, E. (1990) "The communities of science and peer review", *Journal of the American Medical Association*, 263 (10): 1330-2.

Kronick, D. (1990) "Peer review in 18th-century journalism", *Journal of the American Medical Association*, 263: 1321-2.

Lock, S. (1985) *A Difficult Balance, Editorial Peer Review in Medicine.* The Nuffield Provincial Hospitals Trust: London.

Lundberg, G.D. and Williams, E. (1991) "The quality of a medical article, thank you to our 1990 peer reviewers", *Journal of the American Medical Association*, 265 (9): 1161-2.

Marshall, E. (1998) "Medline searches turn up cases of suspected of plagiarism", *Science*, 279: 473-4.

McNutt, R.A., Evans, A.T., Fletcher, R.H. (1990) "The effects of blinding on the quality of peer review", *Journal of the American Medical Association*, 263 (10): 1371-6.

Ong, E.L.C. and Abbott, J. (1991) "Appraising journal's reviewing procedures" (letter), *British Medical Journal*, 302: 1464-5.

Oxman, A.D. (1994) "Checklists for review articles", *British Medical Journal*, 309: 648-51.

Pocock, S.J., Hughes, M.D. and Lee, R.J. (1987) "Statistical problems in the reporting of clinical trials", *The New England Journal Medicine*, 317 (7): 426-32.

Redfern, S.A.T. (1994) "Promoting research into peer review – no quick fixes" (letter), *British Medical Journal*, 309: 538.

Relman, A.S. and Angell, M. (1989) "How good is peer review?", *The New England Journal of Medicine*, 321 (12): 827-9.

Rennie, D. (1989) "Guarding the guardians – a conference on editorial peer review", *Journal of the American Medical Association*, 256 (17): 2391-2.

Rennie, D. (1993) "More peering into editorial peer review", *Journal of the American Medical Association*, 270 (23): 2856-8.

Rennie D, Flanagan A (1994) The second international congress on peer review in biomedical publication", *Journal of the American Medical Association*, 272 (2): 91.

Roberts, J.C., Fletcher, R.H. and Fletcher, S.W. (1994) "Effects of peer review and editing on the readability of articles" in "Annals of Internal Medicine", *Journal of the American Medical Association*, 272 (2): 119-21.

Schulman, K., Sulmasy, D.P. and Roney, D. (1994) "Ethics, economics, and the publication policies of major medical journals", *Journal of the American Medical Association*, 272 (2): 154-7.

Scott, P.V. and Smith, T.C. (1996) "Definition of authorship may be changed – peer reviewers should be identified at end of each publication", (letter), *British Medical Journal*, 313: 821.

Sharp, D.W. (1990) "What can and should be done to reduce publication bias? The perspective of an editor", *Journal of the American Medical Association*, 263 (10): 1390-1.

Scott, P.V. and Smith, T.C. (1996) "Definition of authorship may be changed, peer reviewers should be identified at end of each published paper", *British Medical Journal*, 313: 821.

Smith, R. (1994) "Promoting research into peer review", *British Medical Journal*, 309: 143-4.

Smith, R. (1997) "Peer review – reform or revolution? Time to open up the black box of peer review", *British Medical Journal*, 3 (15): 759-60.

Sweitzer, B.J. and Cullen, D.J. (1994) "How well does a journal's peer review process function? A survey of author's opinions", *Journal of the American Medical Association*, 272 (2): 152-3.

Tonks, A. (1995) "Reviewers chosen by authors – may be better than reviewers chosen by editors", *British Medical Journal*, 311: 210.

Waldron, T. (1992) "Is duplicate publishing on the increase?", *British Medical Journal*, 304: 1029.

Weller, A.C. (1996) "Editorial peer review: a comparison of authors publishing in two groups of US medical journals", *Bulletin of the Medical Library Association*, 84 (3): 359-66.

Williams, N. (1998) "Editors call for misconduct watchdog", *Science*, 280: 1685-6.

Wilson, J.D. (1978) "Peer review and publication", *Journal of Clinical Investigation*, 61: 1697-701.

Wolff, S.P. (1993) "Reform options for peer review" (letter), *Nature*, 364: 183.

Chapter 3

Writing and Computers

by James Hartley

*M*OST people who write today for publication now use word-processors and computer-aided writing programs. Indeed, it is remarkable how much our methods of writing have changed since the late 1980s. In this chapter I wish to consider three aspects of this development. First of all I shall discuss the nature of writing, and how different people go about it. Next, I shall discuss the effects of using computer-aided writing techniques on these procedures. Finally, I shall discuss problems of writing for screen-based as opposed to printed text. My theme throughout will be that writing with and for computers is different from writing without them. I shall argue that new technology not only facilitates many traditional aspects of writing, but that it also changes the nature of writing itself.

The Nature of Writing

Academics read and write a great deal. And the kinds of things that they write vary. Some items are dashed off without much thought – letters home, reminder notes, etc. Some require more painstaking effort – instructions for participants in an experiment, an introduction to an academic paper, a poster for a research presentation, or even an chapter such as this one.

Books and articles about the nature of writing (for example, Hayes, 1996; Hayes and Nash, 1996) typically divide the process of writing into three main, but overlapping, stages. These involve:

- planning: thinking about both the content of the text, and its organisation;

- writing: putting down one's thoughts on paper – or on screen;
- editing: re-thinking and re-planning, as well as correcting spelling errors and the like.

Skilled writers move constantly to and fro between these stages. When we are writing we have to think concurrently about writing neatly (if we are writing by hand); the spelling of some particular words; the grammar and the length of the sentences; how to group these sentences to form complete paragraphs; and how to make these paragraphs cohere to form particular subsections of the text. Also, when writing academic prose, we are likely to have a selection of materials on our desk or nearby (for example, books, previous articles written by ourselves, and articles by others) parts of which might be incorporated into the final product. Small wonder then that writing is a skilled and complex task!

Some researchers (for example, Wason, 1970; Kellogg, 1988) have suggested that in order to improve our writing skills it is helpful to separate out these different aspects of writing. Thus these researchers suggest that during the *planning* stage we should map out the broad issues involved that we wish to cover and the sequence in which we will eventually put them. Often this is done by sketching in a few subheadings. During the *writing* stage they suggest that we should write as quickly as we can, without paying a great deal of attention to punctuation and to spelling, or even to completing sentences. *Editing* can follow later, and this stage too can be subdivided. For example, we might edit first for content, then for grammar and style, and finally check the format of the references.

There are, of course, differences between the ways in which different writers work. In one study Alan Branthwaite and I assessed (by questionnaire) the writing styles of eighty-eight highly productive academic psychologists. By using a statistical method called 'cluster analysis' we were able to describe different kinds of writers. We distinguished between writers (I) in terms of their attitudes and (ii) in terms of their styles of composition. Thus we had 'enthusiastic' or 'anxious' writers, and we had 'doers' (people who got on with it) or 'thinkers' (people who delayed, and wrote multiple drafts). As one might expect, productivity was highest with the 'enthusiastic doers'. Figure 3.1 lists the strategies used by these productive writers which is cast in terms of advice for novices.

Torrance *et al.* (1994) similarly described three kinds of postgraduate writers in the social sciences. In their research these authors distinguished between:

Most productive writers in psychology:

1. Make a rough plan (which they do not necessarily stick to).

2. Complete sections one at a time. (However, they do not necessarily do them in order.)

3. Use a word-processor.

4. Find quiet conditions in which to write and, if possible, write in the same place (or places).

5. Set goals and targets for themselves to achieve.

6. Write frequently – doing small sections at a time – rather than write in long 'binge sessions'.

7. Get colleagues and friends to comment on early drafts.

8. Often collaborate with long-standing colleagues and trusted friends.

Figure 3.1: The characteristic strategies of productive writers in psychology (from Hartley & Branthwaite, 1989)

- 'planners': postgraduates who preferred to have their ideas clear before starting to write, and who produced few drafts;
- 'revisers': postgraduates who preferred to start writing first before taking final decisions about content;
- 'mixed': postgraduates who planned but were then forced to change their plans by repeated revising.

Torrance *et al.* reported that in self-report questionnaires their 'planners' claimed to write more text overall in a given time period than did their 'revisers' and the 'mixed' students. Both the 'planners' and the 'revisers' seemed happy with their writing styles, but members of the 'mixed' group reported more difficulties and anxieties about writing than the other groups.

Studies currently in progress at Birmingham University with under-graduate psychology students also suggest that such students can be grouped into three different kinds of essay writers. Torrance *et al.* (1998) call them:

(1)   'outliners and drafters' – these students typically write a full outline and follow this by writing one or two drafts.

(2)   'drafters' – these students typically write two or more drafts, but do not write full outlines. They may use mental and/or rough notes, however.

(3)   'single drafters' – these students typically produce a single draft which is then corrected for minor errors.

However, it is important to note that the differences between the writers described in these different studies may not be enduring personal traits. The undergraduates studied by Torrance *et al* ., in contrast to those studied by Levy and Ransdell (1996), were not consistent over time (a three-year period). It is likely that people's styles of writing will vary with the task in hand. Presumably easy tasks do not require much planning, whereas difficult ones do. So the simple labels given above do not really do justice to the variety of writing styles that exist (see Chandler, 1995; Eklundh, 1994).

Writing with Computers

The majority of the participants who were involved in the research described above wrote by hand. How will these findings fare when writing is computer-aided?

In this section I shall discuss how new technology can help people plan, write and revise written text. In doing this I find it helpful to think about computer-aided writing programs at three levels of complexity.

Level 1:

Simple programs used for word-processing – making deletions and substitutions, moving paragraphs and sentences about, and printing the text in attractive formats.

Level 2:

More complex programs that add to the above – for example, style, spelling and grammar checkers, and programs that assist with the preparation of indexes and references.

Level 3:

> Even more complex programs that aid writing at a higher level – programs
> that help with the planning and organising of the material.

Level 1 Programs

There has been a great deal of research on using word-processors simply to
process text (see, for example, Haas, 1996). The authors of studies of writing
with word-processors at this level draw attention to:

- How much easier it is (for young children) to write with a keyboard
  than it is with a pen or pencil.
- How much easier it is to read printed rather than hand-written text.
- How much easier it is to make corrections (for example, of spelling)
  on screen, compared with typing or writing with pen and paper.
- How much easier it is to re-sequence, delete and re-write sections of
  text compared with previous methods. Every version looks neat and
  tidy, unlike edited typed or hand-written text.
- How much is lost through this process. Some critics argue that it is
  hard to see or understand the processes involved in writing when
  crossings out, insertions and revised sequences do not appear, and
  when previous versions are eliminated.

Generally speaking the authors of articles about simple word-processors
at all levels of the educational system predict that word-processing will lead
to more drafting, longer texts, and texts of better quality. There is some
evidence to support these claims but much of this evidence is equivocal (see
Bangert-Drowns, 1993; Haas, 1996). Many studies are simply not long
enough, and the participants not practised enough with word-processing
systems for fair comparisons to be made.

Level 2 Programs

More complex computer-aided writing programs assist the composition of
word-processed text in addition to the word-processing of it. Spell checkers
provide a limited example at this level, but grammar and style checkers such
as *Grammatik 5* provide much more sophisticated examples. Figure 3.2 lists
the kinds of errors that *Grammatik 5* detects. Programs such as these can be
run after composing the text, or concurrently whilst writing it.

Early studies of grammar checkers focussed on assessing how useful
individual programs were – particularly for novice writers (for example,

Grammatical errors	Mechanical errors	Stylistic errors
adjective errors	spelling errors	long sentences
adverb errors	capitalisation errors	wordy sentences
article errors	double word	passive tenses
clause errors	ellipsis misuse	end of sentence
comparative/	end of sentence	prepositions
superlative use	punctuation	split infinitives
double negatives	incorrect punctuation	clichés
incomplete sentences	number style errors	colloquialisms
noun phrase errors	question mark errors	Americanisms
object of verb errors	quotation mark misuse	archaic language
possessive misuse	similar words	gender-specific words
preposition errors	split words	jargon
pronoun errors		abbreviation errors
sequence of tense		paragraph problems
errors		questionable word
subject-verb errors		usage
tense changes		

Note: one difficulty with these programs as they currently exist is that you have to have a good working knowledge of grammar to understand them – and this tends to defeat the objective!

Figure 3.2: Examples of different types of errors detected by *Grammatik 5*

Macdonald, 1983). More recent studies have focussed on making comparisons between different programs to see which is the most effective (for example, Kohut and Gorman, 1995). Currently studies seem to be concentrating more on highlighting their deficiencies (for example, Dale and Douglas, 1996; Sydes and Hartley, 1997). Pennington (1993) suggests that grammar checkers should not be used by second-language learners, or by non-proficient writers.

Level 3 Programs
A number of investigators are now considering how programs might be written that will aid the composing process in an even more sophisticated way. In addition to work, for example, on computer-generated abstracts (Paice, 1994) and facilities for translation (A. Hartley and Paris, 1997) researchers are now considering how programs might be written that will aid the planning and the organisational side of writing. Kellogg (1994) for instance discusses three

main difficulties that writers face in connection with this:

(1)   attentional overload – having to cope with too many processes all at once;

(2)   idea bankruptcy – a failure to generate usable ideas;

(3)   anxiety and emotion – which can lead to so-called 'writer's block'.

Kellogg describes a variety of computer programs that help to deal with these fundamental difficulties. 'Funnel' programs channel the writer's attention into only one or two processes at a time; 'inventor' programs help the writer to form and relate concepts; and 'therapist' programs give feedback and reassurance to the writer. Kellogg describes several computer programs under each heading, as well as programs that combine these different functions.

In the United Kingdom work on developing sophisticated programs to help people write is being conducted, amongst others, by Sharples and his colleagues (see Sharples and van der Geest, 1996). Sharples, Goodlet and Pemberton (1989) and Sharples (1994) describe the development of a suite of programs they call *The Writer's Assistant*. This program aims 'to assist the writer throughout the writing process, from the generation and capture of ideas to the production of a connected piece of prose, combining the effects of a text editor, an "ideas processor" and an "outliner" editor'.

The following scenario illustrates how writers might use *The Writer's Assistant:*

A writer wants to produce a study of 'Pottery in North Eastern Brazil' so, on entering the system, she selects the option for creating a new document. As she is writing for a newspaper colour supplement she selects Newspaper Article from a menu of options, getting a structure template and set of constraints appropriate to that type of text. The writer has a fairly firm idea of how the article will fit together, so she starts working in the structure view, sketching an outline for the body of the text by calling up the structure guide to instantiate four main sections headed 'background', 'development of pottery industry', 'evaluation' and 'conclusion'…

With the overall structure established, our writer chooses to brainstorm ideas for the 'development of pottery industry' section. She turns to the notes network view where she sees a note for each of the sections she created in the structural view. She creates notes for subtopics, linking them to the main note with 'aspect' links. To concentrate on one subject – 'description of pottery' – she selects a presentation of the notes network in which that note is displayed in the centre of the screen and then creates further notes to surround it …

The author might then switch to a linear view to find that the system has made an attempt to linearize the notes network into a list of sections and subsections, based on link types. After making some rearrangements she fills out the section headings with text for the article, moving between different perspectives of the linear view to see sections in detail or outlined, until the article is finished. (Sharples *et al.*, 1989)

Computers and Thinking

There is an ongoing debate about whether or not the process of writing affects thinking, and thus whether or not computer-aided writing will change the ways that people write and think. As we saw above, some people argue that writers think first, and then write (the 'thinkers/planners') whilst others argue the reverse of this. They say that people write first and then revise what they have put (the 'doers').

My attention was drawn rather forcefully to this issue some time ago now when I heard that Matthew, a sixteen-year-old acquaintance of mine, had been forbidden by his history teacher to use his word-processor when writing his history essays. Why? Well, the teacher insisted, Matthew would have to write in long-hand when sitting the examination. The teacher argued that the ways of thinking required for writing essays in long-hand under examination conditions were different from those required for writing essays at home with a word-processor.

Was the teacher right? What evidence is there that writing with a word-processor requires different kinds of thinking? I am not sure how one answers questions such as these. There are several possibilities:

- Writing with a word-processor might not involve any changes in processes or any changes in the resulting products.
- Writing with a word-processor might involve some changes in processes, but this may have no obvious effect on the resulting products.
- Writing with a word-processor might involve some changes in processes, and this may lead to some changes (hopefully improvements) in the resulting products.

It seems to me that more sophisticated computer-aided writing programs at levels 2 and 3 described above may indeed alter people's writing processes. But whether or not this changes their ways of thinking is a moot point.

I imagine that the different kinds of writers that I described in the first part of this chapter will start to write with computer-aided writing programs in much the same way as they did before they obtained such aids. However, when they discover what these programs offer, then their strategies may well change. Currently most computer-aided writing programs provide considerable help with the revision processes in writing, so we might expect 'thinkers' to spend more time revising and less time planning than they did before. Similarly, we might expect 'doers' to spend more time planning – with the aid of outlines – than they did initially. Whether or not the resulting products will be different, or of a better quality, is a matter for research. Some tentative beginnings in this direction have been made by Kellogg (1994), Haas (1996) and Zellermayer *et al.* (1991).

This present discussion, of course, is restricted to writers who are starting to use computer-aided writing programs after many years of experience of writing by hand. What the picture will be like with writers who have used computer-aided writing programs from birth, as it were, remains to be seen. One cannot help but think that their ways of writing will be different from ours, especially when keyboards are displaced by voice-input devices (Tucker and Jones, 1991) and dictation becomes fashionable once again (Reece and Cumming, 1996).

Finally, we need to note that so far in this chapter I have concentrated, in the main, on computer-aided writing programs. But it is important not to neglect the fact that new technology impinges on writing in a number of other respects. For example, in writing this chapter I have observed, whilst planning and preparing what I wanted to say, that I have made considerable use of electronic mail (e-mail) and the World Wide Web (WWW). In general (but not particularly for this chapter) I use e-mail:

- to discuss with editors their requirements;
- to help me in my collaboration with other colleagues when we are co-authoring an article;
- to seek additional information from colleagues and friends;
- to send requests for reprints;
- to write letters concerning copyright clearance to authors and publishers;
- to ask for data (usually about writing practices) from e-mail writing groups (for example, by getting them to complete questionnaires).

I use the WWW similarly:

- to find information – from home pages, and listings;
- to find other resources by following links on home-pages;

and I use a fax machine:

- to write letters concerning copyright clearance to authors and publishers, and to send and return proofs.

Thus new technology permeates the writing process.

Writing Screen-based Text

My discussion so far has focussed on writing with computers. In this last section I want to discuss briefly some of the issues that arise when we write for computers – when we write for electronic journals, or when we know that our materials will be produced on screen via e-mail or the WWW.

Of course much of what we know about writing – about how to produce clear text, for example – applies to writing in general and not just to writing for print. Accordingly I have listed some guides for clear writing in an Appendix to this chapter. However, a great deal of the text that we write today is presented on a screen of some kind. We need to think, therefore, of what we can do to help our readers in these new circumstances.

Currently most screen-based text is presented on a screen that differs in orientation from that of the typical printed page. Most screens present their text in a 'landscape' orientation (that is, where the width is greater than the height), whereas most printed text is presented in a 'portrait' orientation (where the width is shorter than the height). Not only do typical screens differ in orientation but they also contains less text than do typical printed pages. (These features, of course, may change: we may soon expect screens big enough to display two A4 pages side by side – and with additional space for other features – and the typography to look little different from print.)

Nonetheless, writers now have to think more in terms of chunks of information that are appropriate to screen-based presentations. A personal example may illustrate the point. Once, when I was writing an article for an electronic journal, I had to make a decision about how to present a large table of results. I had to ask myself whether I should simplify the table to form one 'screenful', or divide it up into three smaller tables? Should I then place these smaller tables in the text or should I place them, or indeed the large one, in an appendix where readers could refer to the information if they wished? Or should I simply omit the original table altogether? I chose in the end to simplify it. Decisions such as these can have unintended consequences. One outcome of writing for small screens is that serious issues might be trivialised.

Structured Text

Another, perhaps more pleasing consequence, might be that articles will have clearer structures. Material that is well structured is easier to read, easier to follow and easier to retrieve, essential requirements for screen-based text. One of the influences of screen-based writing may perhaps be seen in the move to use what are called 'structured abstracts' in medical and psychological journals. Here each abstract typically has subheadings, such as 'Background', 'Aims', 'Methods', 'Results and Conclusions'. Such a format prevents writers from omitting important information, and the consistent format facilitates searching in both printed and electronic databases (Hartley *et al.*, 1996).

Speaking more generally, I have long advocated that when writing both for printed and for screen-based text the underlying structure of a text can be made clearer by the consistent use of appropriate spacing between the elements (see for example, Hartley, 1993; 1994). Figure 3.4 on the following page shows a typical example.

Coloured Text

Not only does new technology furnish us with screens, but it also frequently provides us with a wealth of colour. Today's printed and electronic text can be presented in many different colours on a wide variety of different coloured backgrounds. However, there are several issues to bear in mind when choosing the colours of one's text.

First of all the relevant research suggests, somewhat obviously, that it is wiser to use a dark colour on a light background or a light colour on a dark one. Thus yellow, white and pale blue/green are probably best on a dark background, and black on a light one (Simmonds and Reynolds, 1994). The fact that this is obvious, of course, does not prevent people from ignoring it, particularly on the WWW.

One particular problem with using colour to convey structure in text is that there is no intuitive range of colours to suggest a hierarchy of importance. Thus in presenting text it is best to use few variations in colour, and to use these colours consistently throughout it. Such constraints particularly apply to the design of charts, diagrams, graphs and tables. Here the number of different colours used should be kept to a minimum, they should be used consistently, and they should be clearly differentiated from other colours used in the printed text (Hartley, 1994). One useful tip here might be to think of what the text would look like on a monochrome screen. If the contrast is insufficient then something needs to be done.

Essentially the argument is that one can use multiples of line-space between the elements on the page to help the reader perceive the underlying structure of the text.

Main headings

Units of line-feed can be used consistently to separate out components of the text – such as main, secondary and tertiary headings, paragraphs, and even sentences in complex text.

Secondary headings

One simple way of using line-feed to do this is to use a proportional spacing system.
One can, for example, with complex text start each new sentence on a new line (as here).
One can then separate paragraphs by one extra line space.

One can separate a secondary heading from its ensuing paragraph by providing one extra line space below the heading and two spaces above it. And one can separate main headings from the text by providing two extra line-spaces below the heading and four above it.

If you then feel that the amount of vertical space is excessive, then the scheme can be modified, as in this column. Here I have not started new sentences on new lines, and I have not used a line of space below a secondary heading (and only used one above it). I have now used only one extra line space below a main heading, and two above it. In addition I have added in typographic cues to enhance this spatial arrangement.

Main headings

To repeat, units of line-feed can be used consistently to separate out components of the text – such as main, secondary and tertiary headings.

Secondary headings
The point is that whatever system of spacing is decided upon, it should be used consistently throughout the text. The spacing between the elements should not vary from page to page.

Tertiary headings. Readers particularly like the arrangement shown in the left-hand column when the material in the text is complex, but it probably needs a wider line-length than that used here to show it to its best advantage.

Figure 3.4: Two examples of the use of spacing to show structure in text

Concluding Remarks

The major difference for writers writing with and for computers lies in the fact that we now have much greater control over the appearance of the finished product. Gone are the days when writing involved a chain of experts – author – typist – editor – designer – printer – publisher – each adding their own expertise to the finished text. Today some authors take on all of these roles single-handed.

There are of course advantages and disadvantages in these changes. New technology has profoundly changed the roles of the people in each of these professions. Furthermore, it is probably true to say that authors, on their own, do not have the skills that these professionals do. Nonetheless, with practice and feedback, writers can aspire to match them. And, because writers are attempting to produce final products, they have greater personal involvement than before.

Appendix: Guidelines for Clear Academic Writing

(1) Keep in mind your reader.

Imagine that you are writing for a fellow colleague, or for one of your students – one who is familiar with the conventions of your discipline, but who does not know your area. The reader needs to be able to grasp what you have done, what you have found out, and to follow your argument without undue effort.

(2) Use simple wording.

It is easier to understand short, familiar words than technical terms meaning the same thing. It is probably better to write something like, 'We cannot assume from the start …' than it is to say, 'We cannot assume, *a priori*, … '.

(3) Avoid using too many abbreviations.

Many writers abbreviate technical terms: e.g. RAE (Research Assessment Exercise). Text which is full of abbreviations is off-putting. Furthermore, if the abbreviations are unfamiliar, it is easy to forget what they stand for. (I suggest that you examine your computer centre literature for typical examples.)

(4) Vary your sentence lengths.

It is easier to understand short sentences than long ones because long sentences overload the memory system. Short sentences do not. However, some variation in sentence length is appropriate as otherwise strings of short sentences feel 'choppy'.

As a rule of thumb I suggest that sentences less than 20 words long are probably fine. Sentences 20-30 words long are probably satisfactory. Sentences 30-40 words long are suspect, and sentences with over 40 words in them will probably benefit from re-writing. (The average sentence length of the text in this chapter – stripped of headings, tables, figures and references – is, according to my word-processing package, 17 words long.)

It does not necessarily follow that short sentences are always clear. Many short sentences can turn out to be ambiguous. One of my favourite examples appeared on an application form at Keele University as 'Give previous experience with dates'. One candidate wrote, 'Moderately successful in the past, but I am now happily married.'

(5) Use short paragraphs.

Other things being equal, short paragraphs are easier to read than long ones. However, as with the suggestion about short sentences, some variation in paragraph length is probably desirable. Any article that has a page of text without at least one new paragraph needs attention!

(6) Use active tenses if possible.

Generally speaking, it is easier to understand text when writers use active rather than passive tenses. Compare 'We found that psychologists were more variable than sociologists' with 'For psychologists, compared with sociologists, greater variation was found.' My word-processing package seems to suggest (sorry *suggests*) that I use a lot of passive constructions.

(7) Avoid negatives.

Text is clearer when writers avoid negatives, especially double or treble ones. Negatives can be confusing. I once saw, for example, a label on a lathe in a school workshop which read, 'This machine is dangerous: it is not to be used only by the teacher.' Negative qualifications can be used, however, for particular emphasis, and for correcting misconceptions. Negatives in imperatives (for example, 'Do not ... unless ...') are easily understood.

(8) Place sequences in order.

There are many ways of sequencing text but, whichever way you choose, the presentation needs to have a clear order. Often it is best to describe procedures in the order in which they take place. For example, instead of saying 'Before the machine is switched on, the lid must be closed and the paper placed in the compartment' it would be better to say 'Place the paper in the compartment and close the lid before switching on the machine'.

(9) Use numbers or bullets.

Numbers or 'bullets' are useful if you want to make a series of points within a paragraph. Thus one might re-write the sentence below:

'Four devices to help the reader of a thesis are skeleton outlines for each chapter, headings in the text, a concluding summary and a detailed contents page'

as follows:

'Four devices which help the reader of a thesis are:

- skeleton outlines for each chapter;
- headings in the text;
- a concluding summary; and
- a detailed contents page.'

It is probably best to use *numbers* when there is an order, or sequence in the points being made. *Bullets* are more appropriate when each point is of equal value.

(10) Use structural devices to make the 'organisation' clear.

Writers use several devices to help clarify the structure and the sequence of text. 'Beginning', 'interim' and 'end summaries' can be helpful.

Headings help the reader to scan, select and retrieve material, as well as to recall it. Label the sections so that writers and readers know where they are, and where they are going. Headings can be written in the form of statements or in the form of questions. If the headings are in the form of questions then the text below must answer them, and this helps the reader to follow the argument.

Numbering the headings (and indeed the paragraphs) can also be helpful, although sometimes the numbering of paragraphs can get overdone.

(11) When in difficulty …

If you find it difficult to explain something, think of how you would explain it to someone else. Think of what you would say, try saying it, and then write this down. Then polish it.

(12) Try reading the text out aloud …

Reading the text out loud, or silently to oneself, is a useful way of seeing how well the text flows. You may find that you need to insert commas to make text groupings clearer, that you may get out of breath because sentences are too long, and that you might inadvertently read out a simpler version of the written text. If you do this, change the text to this simpler version.

(13) Ask other people to read your drafts.

Colleagues, and indeed students, may be willing to read and comment on drafts. It can be useful to ask them to point out sentences or sections that other readers might find difficult to follow. People are much more willing to point out difficulties for other people than they are to admit to having such difficulties themselves.

References

Bangert-Drowns, R.L. (1993) "The word-processor as an instructional tool: a meta-analysis of word-processing in writing instruction", *Review of Educational Research*, 63 (1): 69-93.

Chandler, D. (1995) *The Act of Writing.* Aberystwyth: University of Wales.

Dale, R. and Douglas, S. (1996) "Two investigations into intelligent text processing" in M. Sharples and T. van der Geest (eds.) *The New Writing Environment – Writers at Work in a World of Technology.* London: Springer.

Eklundh, K.S. (1994) "Linear and non-linear strategies in computer-based writing", *Computers and Composition*, 11: 203-216.

Haas, C. (1996) *Writing Technology: Studies on the Materiality of Literacy.* Mahwah, N.J.: Erlbaum.

Hartley, A. and Paris, C. (1997) "Multilingual document production: from support for translating to support for authoring", *Machine Translation*, 12: 109-29.

Hartley, J. (1984) "The role of colleagues and text editing programs in improving text", *I.E.E.E. Transactions on Professional Communication, P-C*, 27: 42-4.

Hartley, J. (1993) "The layout of computer-based text" in R. Sassoon (ed.) *Computers and Typography.* Oxford: Intellect.

Hartley, J. (1994) *Designing Instructional Text.* (3rd edn) London: Kogan Page.

Hartley, J. & Branthwaite, A. (1989) "The psychologist as wordsmith: a questionnaire study of the writing strategies of productive British psychologists", *Higher Education*, 18: 423-52.

Hartley, J., Sydes, M. and Blurton, A. (1996) "Obtaining information accurately and quickly. Are structured abstracts more efficient?", *Journal of Information Science*, 22: 349-56.

Hayes, J.R. (1996) "A new framework for understanding cognition and effect in writing" in C.M. Levy and S. Ransdell (eds.) *The Science of Writing.* Mahwah, N.J.: Erlbaum.

Hayes, J.R. and Nash, J.G. (1996) "On the nature of planning in writing" in C.M. Levy and S. Ransdell (eds.) *The Science of Writing.* Mahwah, N.J.: Erlbaum.

Kellogg, R.T. (1988) "Attentional overload and writing performance: effects of rough draft and outline strategies", *Journal of Experimental Psychology: Learning, Memory and Cognition*, 14: 355-65.

Kellogg, R.T. (1994) *The Psychology of Writing*. New York: Oxford University Press.

Kohut, G.F. and Gorman, K.J. (1995) "The effectiveness of leading grammar/style software packages in analyzing business students' writing", *Journal of Business and Technical Communication*, 9: 341-61.

Levy, C.M. and Ransdell, S. (1996) "Writing signatures" in C.M. Levy and S. Ransdell (eds.) *The Science of Writing*. Mahwah, N. J.: Erlbaum.

Macdonald, N.H. (1983) "The UNIX Writer's Workbench software: rationale and design", *Bell System Technical Journal*, 62: 1891-908.

Paice, C. (1994) "Automatic abstracting" in A. Kent (ed.) *Encyclopaedia of Library and Information Science*. (vol. 3, supplement, 16). New York: Dekker.

Pennington, M.C. (1993) "Computer-assisted writing on a principled basis: the case against computer-assisted text analysis for non-proficient writers", *Language and Education*, 7: 43-59.

Reece, J.E. and Cumming, G. (1996) "Evaluating speech-based composition methods: planning, dictating and the listening word processor" in C.M. Levy and S. Ransdell (eds.) *The Science of Writing*. Mahwah, N.J.: Erlbaum.

Sharples, M. (1994) "Computer support for the rhythms of writing", *Computers and Composition*, 11: 217-26.

Sharples, M., Goodlet, J. and Pemberton, L. (1989) "Developing a writer's assistant" in N. Williams and P. Holt (eds.) *Computers and Writing*. Oxford: Intellect Books.

Sharples, M. and van der Geest, T. (eds.) (1996) *The New Writing Environment: Writers at Work in a World of Technology*. London: Springer.

Simmonds, D. and Reynolds, L. (1994) *Data Presentation and Visual Literacy in Medicine and Science*. Oxford: Butterworth-Heinemann.

Sydes, M. and Hartley, J. (1997) "A thorn in the Flesch: observations on the unreliability of computer-based readability formulae", *British Journal of Educational Technology*, 28: 143-5.

Torrance, M., Thomas, G.V. and Robinson, E.J. (1994) "The writing strategies of graduate research students in the social sciences", *Higher Education,* 27: 379-92.

Torrance, M., Thomas, G.V. and Robinson, E.J. (1998) "Strategies for academic writing: individual differences in the writing behaviour of undergraduate students". (In preparation: copies available from G.V. Thomas, School of Psychology, Birmingham University, B15 2TT.)

Tucker, P. and Jones, D.M. (1991) "Voice as interface: an overview", *International Journal of Human-Computer Interaction*, 3: 145-70.

Wason, P. (1970) "On writing scientific papers", *Physics Bulletin*, 21: 407-8. (Reprinted in J. Hartley (ed.) (1980) *The Psychology of Written Communication: Selected Readings*. London: Kogan Page.)

Zellermayer, M., Salomon, G., Globerson, T. and Givon, H. (1991) "Enhancing writing related metacognitions through a computerized writing partner", *American Educational Research Journal*, 28: 373-91.

Chapter 4

The Process of Writing a Scientific Paper

by Glyn V. Thomas

I F you find writing difficult, you are not alone. Surveys have generally found that even academics find writing can be a struggle, and suffer from 'writer's block' from time to time (Hartley and Knapper, 1984). As a consequence of the difficulties they experience, some people come to dislike writing intensely. In a survey of experimental psychologists, Wason (1985) found that dislike of writing was far more common than dislike of reading or talking.

It is not at all obvious why writing can be so difficult. A survey by Hartley and Branthwaite (1989) of highly productive academic writers suggested interesting individual differences. Some respondents in this survey seemed able to write with a minimum of prior planning and subsequent revising. These highly efficient writers Hartley and Branthwaite labelled 'doers'. In contrast, the remaining writers were labelled 'thinkers' because they planned and/or revised their work extensively, devoting a lot of time to thinking about and reflecting on the emerging text.

In this chapter you will find suggestions aimed more at enhancing your productivity as a writer, rather than at improving the style or clarity of your text. The material is grouped into three main sections:

(1) a theoretical background to the nature of writing itself;
(2) the practical steps involved in writing a paper;
(3) the methods writers use to produce text.

The Nature of Writing

A traditional commonsense view of writing is that it involves the expression of meaning in words. This view, which we can call the classical approach to writing, assumes that what you want to say, and how you say it, are two quite separate matters (see Elbow, 1973; Wason, 1970, 1985), implying that you first decide what to write then you choose the words with which to express it.

Many authors of 'self-help' books on how to write have implicitly adopted the classical model. Consequently, they tend to regard the generation and ordering of ideas as a necessary preliminary to, but not part of, the writing process. The advice they offer, therefore, is almost exclusively concerned with the expression of meaning in words. Writers are enjoined, for example, to use short words rather than long, to prefer the active voice to the passive, to use concrete words rather than abstract ones, and so forth. Although this is all good advice, it is of little help in overcoming 'writer's block' or improving your productivity.

Furthermore, an unthinking acceptance of the classical model can lead to trouble in several ways. First, the classical model creates the expectation in the author that writing should be easy if you know your material thoroughly. When you find, as many do, that writing can be extremely difficult, then you feel guilty and inadequate, with the common result that writing becomes even more of a struggle.

Second, adoption of the classical model leads naturally to the suggestion that a thorough knowledge of the topic in question should foster good, clear, writing. However, much evidence suggests that thorough knowledge of a subject is no guarantee of clarity in writing about it. Research students, who are generally thoroughly knowledgeable about their own research, for example frequently experience difficulties in writing their theses (see Torrance *et al.*, 1992; Wason, 1974).

Third, the classical model fosters the expectation that writing should be a linear progression through the stages of planning, composing text, and, finally, revising (Rohman, 1965). In practice, only a few writers work in this way. For most, writing is a recursive process; with planning, composing and revising all extensively interwoven (see, for example, Hartley and Knapper, 1984; Hartley and Branthwaite, 1989). Further difficulties may arise if writers mistakenly come to regard recursive aspects of their activities as signs of inadequacy.

The discrepancies between expectations derived from the classical model and the actual practice of writing suggest that the classical approach may, for many, be based on incorrect assumptions about their writing and thinking processes. As an alternative to the classical view, the generative model of writing has been proposed independently by Elbow (1973) and Wason (1970, 1985). Unlike the classical model, the generative model assumes that meaning and words cannot be neatly separated. In writing, therefore, the task is not so much the translation of meaning into words, as the generation of meaning by writing, (see also Beaugrande, 1984). Consistent with this suggestion, Lowenthal and Wason (1977) found that although some academic writers planned their ideas before writing, there were many who reported that they needed to write in order to think.

Apart from the classical-generative dimension, Hartley and Knapper (1984) found that authors also varied in how they structured the task of writing. Specifically, some authors (often in the arts and humanities) worked holistically, often writing a full first draft at one sitting. Other authors (usually science writers) typically wrote one component at a time and built up their text 'brick by brick'.

Steps to Writing a Paper

Many problems experienced by writers may be due to the (unconscious) adoption of an inappropriate model of the writing process. Accordingly, I will now review various stages of writing a paper in the light of both the classical and generative approaches.

The Plan

According to the classical model the natural starting point for writing is to plan in detail what to say, possibly with the help of a written outline. Only when satisfied with the structure and the sequence of ideas set out in the plan should you begin to look for words to express your meaning.

Alternatively, according to the generative model, you should prepare a first draft in which the important point is to keep writing going, without any corrections or pauses to think about what to say. The result, according to Wason (1985), is the generation of meaning. You discover what you want to say in the process of writing. The generative view is that a detailed plan is unnecessary, and may even be counter-productive.

Elbow (1973) considers generative writing to involve two important processes, 'growing' and 'cooking'. Writing many drafts provides the opportunity for 'growing', that is, the generation of meaning. Re-reading and revising those drafts, and showing them to others for comments, comprises 'cooking', that is, a process of interactions. To allow these interactions to work, it is important not to have too rigid a plan, but to allow your material to evolve.

I am not suggesting that you start to write with a completely 'blank' mind. It is desirable (and inevitable) that you will start to write with at least some ideas and a sense of a structure. There are also important external constraints on writing a paper, such as its organisation into sections. In order to conform to the required format some preliminary analysis and identification of the purpose of each section is essential (see below).

While not everyone will agree that you should never write to a plan, it is clear from a generative point of view that plans should be used only as a starting point for writing. Research suggests that, in practice, writing frequently departs from a prepared plan. Kaufer *et al.* (1986) found that even those writers who produced the most detailed of plans introduced, on average, eight times more ideas in their final text than were listed in the original plan. Sticking with an inappropriate plan can also be a problem. Rose (1980), for example, concluded that writers who suffer most from writer's 'block' appear to have more difficulty departing from plans than other writers.

A particular advantage of the generative approach is that questions of sequencing can be postponed until after completion of a first draft. Once a draft has been prepared, the structure and sequence of arguments and ideas can be handled spatially on paper; which is often much easier than trying to arrange them in one's head during pre-planning. With the development of word-processing computers, quite radical re-ordering of a draft can be executed with ease.

Composing Strategies

For most of us it is unrealistic to expect our first drafts to be totally satis-factory. Knowing that your text will pass through several drafts, however, does allow you to develop a strategy to maximise your efficiency. It might be time-efficient, for example, to concentrate on generating content in initial drafts by deliberately neglecting requirements of correct English and good style. Both Wason and Elbow advise that in order to maximise the potential for generating ideas when writing, you should produce your first draft without pauses for reflection or to make changes or corrections. This process externalizes meaning and creates opportunities for new ideas to emerge.

> As I start to write, things come together, particularly in writing an essay. Writing these thoughts down as I go leads to other thoughts which I then write down. The examination of words leads to new thoughts. (Wason, 1985)

Subsequent drafts provide opportunities to re-order material to achieve the best sequence of ideas, and to revise the text in order to correct punctuation and spelling, and to improve the style.

Rough drafting like this can also be a solution to the notorious problem of 'writers's block' when concern over what to say and how to say it combine to inhibit productivity. Writing a first draft however roughly at least gets one started by postponing concerns over the selection of material, sequence and presentation. Many writers have maintained that in these circumstances it is most important to keep writing something, no matter how inadequate or inappropriate you may feel it to be. A related problem is that of getting started on writing, often because of the fear of seeming foolish or of writing something ridiculous. Again, lowering expectations for that first crucial draft can be particularly helpful in getting writing underway (see Torrance *et al.*, 1993). At the heart of all these rough drafting recommendations is the belief that it is nearly always easier to improve on a deficient first draft than it is to start writing in the first place.

Revising

From the point of view of the classical approach to writing, revising should constitute only a minor part of your total writing effort. Its function is largely cosmetic: correcting spelling and punctuation and introducing minor changes of phrasing. This kind of revising is closer to what publishers call 'copy-editing', where the aim is not to change the meaning of the texts, but to ensure clarity of expression and consistency of style. From the classical standpoint, extensive revisions are symptoms of inadequate planning, and are, therefore, to be deprecated.

In a generative approach to writing, however, revising is a major part of the thinking/writing process. Far from being a sign of poor writing, extensive revisions are to be expected as essential and productive aspects of good writing. Hartley and Knapper (1984) quoted Liam Hudson's experience (see Cohen, 1977) to illustrate this approach:

> I rewrite everything. I do, in practice, at least nine or ten drafts. The first things I do are always ridiculous. They don't come to life until I redraft them many times. For instance, I've just written what I think will be an eighty thousand word book, and I will have written well over a million words to get that.

Research into the way writers revise their text indicates that experienced writers consider large units and global patterns more than do inexperienced writers. Experienced professional adult writers studied by Sommers (1980) reported that their first aim in revising was to find the form or shape of their argument. One of her subjects reported: 'My first draft is very scattered. In rewriting, I find the line of the argument. After the argument is resolved, I am much more interested in word choice and rephrasing.' In contrast, Sommers found that most college students regarded revising primarily as a re-wording activity, in which individual words only were exchanged. Similarly Torrance *et al.* (1992) found that only a minority of postgraduate students reported making major changes to the meaning and structure of their texts during revision.

Another aspect of revision on which experts and novices often differ is in sensitivity to the needs of readers. Sommers (1980) found that experienced writers often imagine someone else reading their text and try to anticipate that reader's reactions. These anticipations of readers' judgments are then often the stimulus for further revision. In contrast, novice writers appear to have difficulty in constructing readers' likely reactions.

Hayes and Flower (1986) suggest that writers' knowledge of their own texts make it difficult for them to detect faults. The writer's own knowledge, for example, may automatically supply the missing steps in the arguments and clarify the ambiguities in the wording. Such a process could partly explain why it is often much easier to identify faults in other writers' texts than in one's own! Consistent with this hypothesis, Hayes and Flower (1986) describe how readers with prior knowledge of the subject matter of an unclear text identified significantly fewer of the faults in it than did naïve readers.

Given that prior knowledge of subject matter interferes with the diagnosis of faults necessary for successful revision, then there is much to be gained by inviting others to read your text and to comment upon it. Hayes and Flower (1986) note that inviting naïve readers to 'think aloud' as they attempt to understand a piece of text may be an especially efficient way of identifying problems. If another reader cannot be found then putting the text aside for a time before revising it may be helpful: 'I like then to put the manuscript in a drawer for a couple of weeks ... then on returning to it I can read it with greater objectivity ...' (from Hartley and Knapper, 1984).

Organisation, Structure and Style

Scientific papers can be review articles, theoretical articles, or reports of original research; and each of these requires a different kind of content and internal structure. In general, it is important to clarify precisely the purpose of each section of the paper. Note that readers in different disciplines will have their own distinct expectations about the content, organisation and style of papers in their field. Not all these expectations will be adequately conveyed even by a comprehensive set of authors' instructions, such as those issued by most journal editors. Consequently, it may be helpful to read several articles from past issues of a journal to which you plan to submit your paper, in order to discover some of these implicit expectations. The following remarks concern some of the more common problems of content, organisation and style encountered in writing scientific papers.

The title is the most frequently read part of a paper, and, very often, it may be the only part that is read. It is also of considerable bibliographic importance because it is used as a statement of a paper's content for indexing and for abstracting and information services. Hence it is worth giving some time and effort to achieve the best possible result. The title should be a concise statement of the main topic and should identify the variables and/or theoretical issues under consideration.

An abstract should be a brief but comprehensive summary of the contents of the article. Like the title it is often the only part of the paper that may be read. It should be self-contained, concise and specific. Especially if you write generatively, it may be wise to leave the abstract until you have written the rest of the paper, and have thereby discovered what your paper is really about!

The introduction to a scientific paper should present the background to the specific issue under study. Swales and Najjar (1987) have suggested that many introductions to scientific research articles can be seen as a series of 'moves' developing a scientific argument:

(1)   Establish the field. State the field in which your research lies, and why that field is interesting and important.
(2)   Selectively review previous research leading up to the present research.
(3)   Indicate the gap in present knowledge and/or understanding that the present research will fill.
(4)   Explain how your chosen methods and research design will produce data that will fill the gap identified in (3) above.

The method section of a research report should describe in detail what you did and how you did it. The information should be sufficient for another investigator to replicate the study if they wish. The rationale for the choice of method can sometimes go into this section, but if extensive it is more usual to locate explanations and justifications in the introduction (see above). In that way, the method section can be preserved as a largely factual summary of procedures. Because it is primarily descriptive, many authors find the method section the easiest part of a paper to write.

The results section of a research report should summarise the data collection and any analyses of them. The main results should be stated briefly, followed by the data in sufficient detail to justify the conclusions. The analyses used should be justified only if their use is unconventional.

The discussion of a research report evaluates the results and discusses their implications for the hypotheses and questions set out earlier in the introduction. A common fault is the unnecessary repetition of results in the discussion section. Another is to develop an overly general theoretical discussion of matters not directly arising from the results. In some disciplines and journals, it is usual to have a short section headed 'Conclusions' at the very end of the paper. To some extent such a conclusions section is simply a summary of the discussion.

Copy-editing

Whichever approach to writing you adopt, your text will almost always benefit from some copy-editing. Copy-editing is concerned with correcting English and improving style. As mentioned above, most books on how to write concentrate on these largely technical matters. Here are some typical examples of the advice on offer:

- Check that the sequence of ideas is orderly.
- Prefer short words and short sentences.
- Avoid jargon and specialised technical terms where possible.
- Delete all unnecessary words and irrelevancies.
- Avoid repetition.
- Use the active voice.
- Use the past tense for conditions or actions that occurred at specific times in the past.
- Use the present tense for actions or conditions that continue into the present.
- Check that statements are unambiguous.
- Avoid any term or expression with 'surplus meaning' e.g., sexist language, terms which convey ethnic bias, and slang.

Most of this advice is obviously aimed at clarity and objectivity. Note also that if you follow this advice, you are likely to reduce the length of your paper, make it more readable, and give it greater impact.

Collaborative Writing

Published writing, especially scientific writing, is seldom a completely solo production. As noted above, texts are nearly always improved by getting others to comment on them. This outside input is often informal, as when colleagues and friends read through drafts, and seeking such feedback is probably the single most effective action that writers can take to enhance their papers. Scientific papers, especially those testing theories and offering inter-pretations of evidence are generally subjected to a reviewing process by journal editors and reviewers. Most writers find that editors and reviewers' reports, though sometimes ego bruising, can also be an invaluable source of advice for improving their papers. Indeed, in some North American journals, the amount of editorial feedback is often so substantial that the editors and reviewers have become ghost co-authors of the paper.

In many areas of science, papers with multiple authors have become the norm. Of course, multiple authorship need not mean that every named author has necessarily played a significant role in the writing process. Many of the authors may have contributed to the paper in other ways, such as conducting specialised tests on samples. Nevertheless, it is common for the task of writing to be shared by two or more individuals. This can lead to disagreements about the relative contribution of each, and who should be first author. Such matters are really beyond the scope of the present chapter, but it may be worth saying that where material is extensively revised and re-written the precise contri-bution of each of several collaborating authors can be virtually impossible to disentangle. A common convention is that the first author should prepare the first draft.

It is worth noting that the array of editing facilities provided by computers make collaborative writing much easier (always assuming that the collabora-ting authors have compatible computers and software!). Using specialised adaptations, some writers have collaborated by working together on the same document at the same time. The idea is that in addition to the unique contribu-tion that each partner makes, there is an added advantage that the suggestions made by one may trigger new ideas in the other. Hence the interest in arrange-ments that maximise interactions between the collaborators. As you might expect, the success of such partnerships seems to depend a lot on the personalities of the collaborators.

Methods of Producing Text

It is still the case that there are four basic methods writers can use to produce text: they can write in long hand, they can use a typewriter or a word-processing computer, or they can dictate. It is safe to assume that writing in long hand and using a computer are currently the two most frequently chosen options for academic and scientific writing. In the past dictation was not a popular option for academics and scientists, perhaps because of the lack of secretarial help to transform the dictated material into a text. Hartley and Knapper (1984) in their survey of British and Canadian academic writers found that dictation was used in the early stages of writing by only three out of sixty-three respondents. Dictation may become more popular in the future now that products have become available that allow writers to dictate text directly into their computer. Currently, most such systems require discrete pauses between the speaking of successive words which some users have found breaks up the flow of their thought. With further development and refinement, however, such voice entry systems may offer the writer many advantages for some kinds of writing.

Although typewriters were once a popular choice for many writers, they have been all but totally displaced by computers. Perhaps the most obvious advantages of a computer over other methods for writing are its elimination of much of the physical labour involved in correcting and revising text, and the enormous range of options it offers for different formats and styles of printed copy.

The impressive range of output options, however, can be something of a distraction. Far more important are the many ways in which computers facilitate the revising and editing of text. In this regard, word-processing computers seem to have been designed to facilitate generative approaches to writing which require repeated revisions and re-writing. There are also implications for how the task of writing is structured and perceived. Given that the text displayed on the screen and held in the computer may exist in any one particular form only briefly, then the definition of what counts as a draft changes significantly.

It is also possible that once writers appreciate that revisions and corrections are easy to implement with a computer then, in generating text, they will be able to concentrate more on the meaning of their writing than on the technical aspects of presentation, spelling, grammar, and so forth. In practice, however, it seems to be all too easy to become seduced into fiddling around with exotic fonts and the surface presentation of the text, at the expense of considering the meaning of the text and its deeper structure. When writing or revising for meaning it may be best to select a display that allows you to view as large a section of text as possible, so as to facilitate consideration of meaning at a global as well as a local level.

Because of the greater legibility of a clean printed copy over one written in long hand, computers (like typewriters) also offer the advantage that it is easy for others to read and comment on early drafts of the text. Daiute (1983) has suggested that using a computer also facilitates evaluation of changes to a piece of text. Corrections made by hand involve crossing out words and adding inserts between lines, and it may be difficult for the writer/reader to consider them as an integral part of the text. In contrast, a text editor can incorporate changes smoothly into the rest of the piece, and, consequently, it may be easier to consider the revised text as a whole.

Daiute (1983) has also claimed that using a computer can have psychological advantages over writing by hand. The computer, she suggests, may seem like an 'audience' and thus help the writer to take the reader's point of view. Another benefit is that entering text into the computer can involve less commitment of effort than writing the same text by hand. As a consequence, writers may feel freer to experiment, and to explore many more potential themes in their writing. Daiute (1983: 143) reports that writers also experience fewer 'blocks when using a computer ... the computer freed them because the computer's page is not so permanent; it's so easy to change'.

Writing with a computer can have additional advantages at the copy-editing stage. Not only can corrections be easily made using the text editor, there are also supplementary programmes available which will check the text automatically for common spelling mistakes, query aspects of your grammar and style, and even provide a thesaurus for alternative words. That said, grammar and spelling checkers seem not to be as widely used as you might expect. In part these aids may be resisted because of their undoubted limitations. Spelling checkers, for example, notoriously test the spelling of each word taken in isolation, and are no guarantee that the words make sense in the context of a sentence.

I have a spelling checker,
It came with my PC.
It plainly marks four my revue
Mistakes I cannot sea.
I'm sure your please to no,

It's letter perfect in it's weigh,
My checker tolled me sew.

(Source unknown)

Spelling and grammar checkers can also be very irritating to use. Spelling checkers generally query unusual names (in reference lists) and specialised scientific terms that are common in particular fields of study. The result is that the check often proceeds only slowly with a great many false alarms. To counter this problem, most good spell checkers allow you to add special names and terms to their lexicons. Grammar checkers can also generate an inordinate number of false alarms, repeatedly querying, for instance, every use of 'affect' and 'effect', 'principle' and 'principal', and protesting at every long sentence. Nevertheless, viewed simply as aids, and not substitutes for proper copy-editing and proof reading, such software assistants can be real time-savers and reduce the number of technical errors in your text.

Some publishers of scientific journals have developed programmes which also help writers to produce their paper in accord with the 'house-style' of the publisher. These manuscript preparation programmes, amongst other things, prompt the correct entry of each element of a reference; automatically number tables, figures and footnotes; check that each citation has a reference and *vice versa*; and prompt the correct use of heading levels. The 'paper' can also be submitted in electronic form on a computer disk, saving time and effort and reducing type setting errors.

Given all these advantages, it may seem surprising that there is anyone still writing in long hand. It is clear, however, that not everyone takes to writing with computers. Changing long established practices and methods always seems to involve an initial loss of competence, which may seriously inhibit change. A few of my own colleagues, for example, report that despite many attempts to compose text at a keyboard, they find they can still only generate sentences when writing in long hand. The resulting text is then typed into a word-processor for final corrections and printing.

Studies of less experienced writers have also found that newcomers to writing with computers spontaneously make only limited use of the editing potential of their machines. Hawisher (1987), for example, found that the revision strategies of college students and the quality of their writing were not necessarily enhanced when they wrote with computers.

Hawisher noted that revising on the screen of a computer may actually inhibit global revisions because most computer screens display only small segments of text at a time. When writing with a computer, therefore, it may be crucial to undertake at least some revising on a printed copy of the text so that the sequence of ideas and the overall structure of the text can be more readily perceived. When the use of computers for significant revision of text has been specifically built into the instruction that students receive, however, then the results of using computers for writing have been more positive. For example,

Bernhardt *et al.* (1989) found significantly better quality of writing in students using computers, which they attributed directly to the more extensive revisions undertaken by the computer trained students (see also Chapter 3 by Hartley in this volume).

In addition to facilitating the revision and polishing of text, computers can be used to assist with other aspects of the writing process. There have been, for instance, several attempts to provide computer-based support for collecting and generating content for texts, and for planning and structuring that content into an orderly sequence of ideas (again, see Chapter 3). In terms of collecting information prior to writing, there is no doubt that it will be increasingly easy for academics and scientists to use their computers to gain access to the Internet and to library databases. New sources of information are constantly emerging, and traditional outlets such as long established journals are now published in electronic as well as printed paper versions. The days of actually leaving your desk and physically visiting a library may soon be little more than a memory!

Most scientists and academics quickly build up a file of references and other similar sources that they use in their work, often as text files in one of the common word-processing systems. It is possible, however, to acquire special software for handling files of references, which offer some advantages when references need to be re-formatted into different styles for different journals, or searched for topic key-words. Against this has to be set the cost of purchasing the software in a form that is compatible with your existing word-processing system, and investing the initial time and effort to transfer all your existing reference indexes into the new system.

The main ways in which computers have been configured to provide help with organising, thinking about, and planning text is in the provision of an 'outliner'. These software systems allow you to switch between composing and editing text to an outline of the main points in your text or a summary of paragraph and section headings. It is true that writers need to consider their text at several levels, and switch between levels repeatedly during composing and revising (Beaugrande, 1984). Consequently, we can expect that outliners may well be useful to the writers who take the trouble to learn how to use them. Others may find that it is easier just to keep an outline in their mind or handwritten on a piece of paper.

There has been much written and said about the ways in which computers, the Internet and World Wide Web will change communication among scientists (and everyone else), and lead to the demise of traditional journals and books. Associated with these speculations is often the suggestion that hypertext, allowing non-linear progression through electronically interconnected networks of text 'pages', will replace the familiar linearly organised text of paper-based publications.

Just a few reflections seem in order. First, there are important and fundamental aspects of writing and of text which seem to be independent of the medium of presentation. Within hypertext, for example, the elements of text need to have a coherent linear internal structure, and to link coherently to the various other elements within the hypertext 'document'. These requirements for internal coherence and connectedness seem to be little different in principle from the requirements placed on the component parts of conventional scientific papers. In fact, writing for Web pages and hypertext documents can be much harder than writing linear text, because there are more constraints to meet with the former. It seems unlikely that the need for clear fluent written communication in science will decline. Furthermore, the demands of producing scientific text, however it is presented, will still involve the generation of content and meeting the requirements of good English and clear expression. Writing on a computer may look on the surface to be a very different activity from writing with pen and paper. Beneath the surface, however, the cognitive demands and processes may have much in common.

Second, it may be a mistake to assume that traditional texts printed on paper as books or journals are inherently linear. It hardly needs to be said that readers scan printed texts, and read selectively. Actually, scanning and selective reading can often be performed more easily on a printed paper document than on a computer screen. Given also that text pages accessed *via* an Internet connection generally take appreciable time to transfer, old fashioned ink and paper can often be more 'reader friendly'. There is a possible link (*sic*) to be made here with the experience of revising documents, in which it often seems easier to apprehend the global structure of a document when working with a printed paper copy than with text displayed only on the computer screen.

One celebrated feature of material distributed *via* the Internet is that it is uncensored and unedited. In the domain of science this means both that publication is freer so that readers have greater access to a wider range of material, but also that they have more dross to sift through before they find something they really want to read. It seems likely that the role of editors and reviewers in selecting (and improving) scientific papers for publication will continue for at least some electronically distributed material. A likely development will be the growth of electronic versions of established journals that originally appeared only in paper form. Other developments such as electronic mail lists and bulletin boards will presumably fill other niches in the information market, such as quick publication of preliminary results or the expression of unorthodox views.

Conclusions

Writing anything more complex than a simple 'Thank you' letter is neither easy nor well understood. We can see, however, the beginnings of a theory of the writing process. Writing is seldom a linear progression from ideas to expression to revising as the classical model suggests. Rather it is a recursive and interactive process in which generation of words and meaning is interwoven with evaluation and revision. An initial analysis of the purpose of a piece of writing is probably essential, but the preparation of a detailed plan may not be necessary for everyone, and may even be counter-productive. Writing a scientific paper is so complex an activity that, for many of us, the task must be broken down into parts so that we can tackle one part at a time. There are various strategies available to help partition these tasks; such as planning, rough drafting, and phased revision. There seems to be no one ideal strategy that will suit everyone or every writing task. Why not reflect on your own writing practices in the light of the information presented here, and experiment with some alternative strategies? The initial investment of effort in reflecting on and varying your writing behaviour may well be repaid not only in better writing, but in more enjoyable writing.

References

Beaugrande, R. de (1984) *Text Production: toward a science of composition.* Norwood, N.J.: Ablex Publishing Corporation.

Bernhardt, S.A., Edwards, P. and Wojahn, P. (1989) "Teaching college composition with computers", *Written Communication*, 6: 108-33.

Cohen, D. (1977) *Psychologists on Psychology.* London: Routledge and Kegan Paul.

Daiute, C.A. (1983) "The computer as stylus and audience", *College and Composition and Communication*, 34: 134-45.

Elbow, P. (1973) *Writing without Teachers.* Oxford: Oxford University Press.

Hartley J., and Branthwaite, A. (1989) "The psychologist as wordsmith: a questionnaire study of the writing strategies of productive British psychologists", *Higher Education*, 18: 423-58.

Hartley, J. and Knapper, C. K. (1984) "Academics and their writings", *Studies in Higher Education*, 9: 151-67.

Hawisher, G.E. (1987) "The effects of word processing on the revision strategies of college freshmen", *Research in the Teaching of English*, 21: 145-59.

Hayes, J.R. and Flower, L.S. (1986) "Writing research and the writer", *American Psychologist*, 41: 1106-13.

Kaufer, D., Hayes, J.R. and Flower, L.S. (1986) "Composing written sentences", *Research in the Teaching of English*, 20: 121-40.

Lowenthal, D. and Wason, P.C. (1977) "Academics and their writing", *The Times Literary Supplement*, 24 June.

Rohman, G. (1965) "Pre-writing: the stage of discovery in the writing process", *College Composition and Communication*, 16: 106-12.

Rose, M. (1980) "Rigid rules, inflexible plans, and the stifling of language: a cognitivist analysis of writer's block. *College Composition and Communication*, 31: 389-401.

Sommers, N. (1980) "Revision strategies of student writers and experienced adult writers", *College Composition and Communication*, 31, 378-88.

Swales, J.M. and Najjar, H. (1987) "The writing of research article introductions", *Written Communication*, 4: 175-92.

Torrance, M.S., Thomas, G.V. and Robinson, E.J. (1992) "The writing experiences of social science research students", *Studies in Higher Education*, 17: 155-67.

Torrance, M.S., Thomas, G.V. and Robinson, E.J. (1993) "Training in research writing: an evaluation of three courses for postgraduate students", *British Journal of Educational Psychology*, 63: 179-84.

Wason, P.C. (1970) "On writing scientific papers", *Physics Bulletin*, 21: 407-8.

Wason, P.C. (1974) "Notes on the supervision of PhD's", *Bulletin of the British Psychological Society*, 27: 25-9.

Wason, P.C. (1985). "How to write an essay", *The New Psychologist*, May, 16-9.

Chapter 5

Illustrations

by Veronica Barnes

Introduction

*T*HE sentences 'Every picture tells a story' and 'A picture is worth a thousand words' emphasise the inadequacy of words alone.

> What is the use of a book … without pictures. (Lewis Carroll)

These may be exaggerated claims but visual images are a very effective form of communication. Used appropriately, illustrations or visuals can enhance the appearance of an academic paper, improving its clarity, coherence and general readability.

This chapter discusses the reasons for using visuals and provides ideas on which to use and where. It will guide you around the different types of visuals which could be used in academic papers. Remember, though, that any paper will inevitably reflect the style of its author, and individual authors will have their own reasons for considering the use of visuals. This chapter will look at what is on offer and what is perceived to be successful. Bear in mind that if illustrations are to be used they should improve the attractiveness of your writing, make it look good and if relevant help to sell it!

Purpose

It has been claimed that as much as 83 per cent of our learning is through sight. Since it is the major sense we should take advantage of it and therefore use it as much as possible. However, an illustration should add something to the written text. It must be worth having, both aesthetically and financially – it should be worthy of its place. An illustration should complement the written word and not be a repeat of it. It must be informative and relevant. The financial cost of using illustrations should not be disregarded. Illustrations may be quite expensive, involving graphic artist fees and copyright fees for example.

Picture the infant, paintbrush in hand communicating through pictures. As our education progresses our efforts at school are concentrated on reading and writing. Unfortunately the vast majority of us then lose the natural ability to draw, and as adults writing academic papers, illustrating them becomes quite alien and requires enormous thought to be achieved successfully. Perhaps we should remember our ancestors communicating via drawings on cave walls, such as those at Lascaux in France.

Figure 5.1: Sketch of a typical cave painting

Illustrations are put into a text to help the reader to understand or visualise something more easily and by so doing enhance the learning outcome of the publication. Visuals can also give movement to an action or process; for example, one can use a flowchart to describe a process which is quite difficult to describe in words. If well-prepared, they can also be eye-catching and memorable.

Good visuals also break up the written words and can be visually appealing. We know there is nothing more daunting than pages and pages of unbroken text. Once upon a time there was a simple rule about having one illustration per 1,000 words placed half way down the relevant text, but today with advanced technology, desktop publishing, computerised drawings and the like, there can be much more flexibility.

In short according to Ericson (1987) illustrations can:

Attract	Motivate	Inform
Instruct	Simplify	Explain
Demonstrate	Identify	Discriminate
Entertain	Influence	Enrich
Translate	Correct	Show relationships
Save time	Give variety	Summarise

The watch-word when using illustrations is 'quality' not 'quantity'.

Figure 5.2: Illustrating

You may have the advantage of the use of a graphic artist. In this case it is wise to consult them at each stage of preparation. Their advice should prove invaluable in the sizing and placing of illustrations. This is a two-way process, however, and you should brief them thoroughly so your requirements are fully understood. If you decide to do as much artwork as possible yourself you can draw freehand, use computers, trace or photocopy. The latter allows you to change sizing by enlarging or reducing. It is often useful to work larger than the final illustration and then reduce down. There are also available volumes of copyright-free artwork which you can certainly find in design departments of large institutions and probably in libraries too.

Illustrations

Illustrations represent a symbolic language and you, as an author, need to decide what type of illustrations will best complement your text.

There are any number of different formal classifications of illustrations, but this chapter is not the place to argue for the adoption of any of these. The idea here is to look at the different types of illustrations and note how they can enhance the written word.

Of course you may be writing for many different purposes, perhaps preparing a book or submitting a conference paper. The space available to you will therefore be variable and you will obviously need to take this into account when considering the use of visuals, as will any 'house-style' rules which you may need to adhere to.

Illustrations may vary from a professionally commissioned photograph to a hand-drawn line diagram. What must be remembered is that all visuals should be:

simple
uncluttered
appropriately labelled
clear
a sensible size
complement the text

Half Tones

'Half tones' are photographs and other artwork, for example, paintings or wash drawings which include tones of grey as well as extremes of black and white. They often depict a subject and are more realistic than diagrams, but this type of illustration is usually quite expensive.

If photographs are to be used, then they should be clear and focussed. The subject should stand out against the background. If there is detail in the background the reader will be distracted and not concentrate on the important image on the photograph. Photographs may be in colour or black and white, depending on your budget and any guidelines provided by the publisher or other intended recipient of the paper.

If you are taking your own photographs you must consider the type of camera you plan to use and the type of film (black and white, colour or specialised film). Check your subject is in the right position. Light, whether natural or artificial should enhance the subject and not obscure it. Study the subject imagining the resultant photograph. Do not be too hasty to press the shutter. For some subjects (especially scientific), a suitable scale should be placed in an appropriate position, for example, a coin or ruler or even a person next to the subject.

When you submit these to the publisher, (whether they are prints or negatives) place them carefully in a protected envelope; *never* use paper clips or staples on them as this may cause damage. Remember that unless you are taking or are having taken original photographs you will certainly need formal permission and may need copyright clearance.

Paintings and Drawings

These are frequently used where no photograph exists. They can portray reality or be fictitious. Engineering drawings are very precise and often highly detailed. If therefore you need to include this type of drawing you may have to delete some of the detail. Computerised drawings are very popular today because so many user-friendly packages are available. Many software packages provide tools to draw your own illustration and also provide pre-drawn objects which can be pasted into your text, then all the writer has to do is to give it a label, a border and a caption.

Maps

Maps are used to show locations and spatial relationships. They may be very detailed or quite simple. If you need to place a map in your work, delete any unnecessary detail to avoid confusing the reader. If you require a lot of detail consider having a series of maps to illustrate different features. For example, the series of maps below:

Map 1: The North American Continent – country boundaries

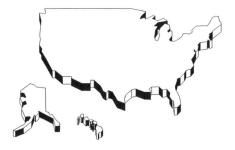

Map 2: North America

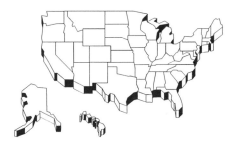

Map 3: The United States of America – state boundaries

Your publisher will expect you to have checked such items as boundaries, scales, orientation, lines of latitude or longitude and the key. Do not assume that a map and caption alone explain what you want!

Maps are one of the illustrations which may need a fold-out or a double page spread. Beware of this! If you are using a double page spread, try and make the divide in the middle but be careful that nothing crucial is lost in the spine. Fold-outs are very expensive and should only be used when absolutely necessary. They are also prone to tearing by readers, which spoils the paper or book.

Figures and Diagrams

Figures and diagrams are line drawings used to explain specific points. They are made up of single lines of equal weighting. They may also be dots or pure black shading. They are usually less realistic and more abstract. They may describe a concept diagrammatically, for example 'Communication' in Figure 5.3 below:

Figure 5.3: 'Communication'

or, they may show how something works or the interaction of a particular system. You will find that figures or diagrams are the most common type of illustration, for example the figure below:

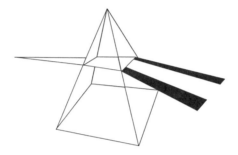

Figure 5.4: White light refracting through a prism

Bear in mind that the word 'diagram' is not generally used today. Most of these types of illustrations are called 'figure'.

Graphs and Charts

Graphs and charts tend to show 'how much', that is, they represent numbers in a visual form.

Graphs

These give an immediate overall picture. There are two main types of graph: conceptual (where shape is the most important factor) and detailed (where numerical information is important). Graphs allow the reader to interpolate between points. They may also be used to extrapolate beyond the last point on the graph, and as such are frequently used for forecasting.

You must always be very clear about the type of scale you are using, that is, is it linear or logarithmic. The axes should be clearly and consistently labelled, and the scale and units indicated if relevant, (it is rarely necessary to reproduce the actual gridlines), but a key should always be provided.

Graphs can be simple as illustrated in Figure 5.5 or more complex when a number of variables are plotted between the same axes.

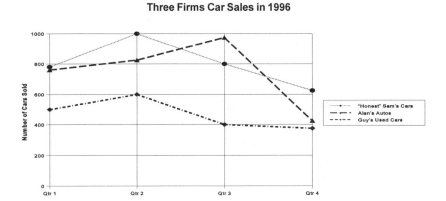

Figure 5.5: Three firms' car sales, 1996

Charts

These also deal with numbers. Two of the most common charts are bar charts and pie charts. The bar chart is used for showing and/or comparing areas, quantities over time etc. (see Figure 5.6).

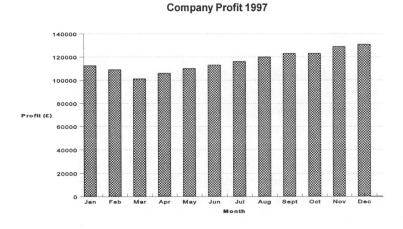

Figure 5.6: Company profit for 1997

Pie charts are commonly used to make comparisons of parts of the whole (see Figure 5.7). The pie chart in this Figure has some shading. Frequently pie charts are filled with different shading or stipple which may make the segments more distinguishable. However, remember that if the stipples are too similar it can cause confusion.

A-level grades achieved at St. Winnifreds School 1997

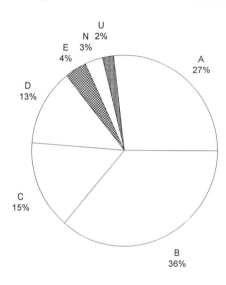

Figure 5.7: 'A' Level grades at St. Winnifreds, 1997

Tables

Tables tend to fall between categories, for while they are text they are also illustrations. Often it is more sensible to explain numbers in a table rather than in text using words, since a table is useful for condensing data. You must try to ensure that tables are never split because this is very irritating for the reader. They also need to be close to the relevant text though details should not be repeated in text as this defeats the whole object of creating a table.

If you have to use a number of tables, you should make sure that the style and structure is consistent for each. Column headings should be clearly labelled, as should row stubs heading (see Table 5.1), and units must be clear if the table is illustrating quantities. Tables may well become very complicated, but this is perfectly acceptable provided that each one is well structured.

Tables normally have titles rather than captions and you must make sure that these are clear.

▸Table 1. Local snack survey◂ TITLE

	▸**Name**◂ COLUMN HEADING		
▸**Food type**◂ STUB HEADING			
	Brian	**Fred**	**Susan**
Crisps	Salt and Vinegar	Ready Salted	Cheese and Onion
Sweets	Jelly Babies	Liquorice	Fruit Pastilles
Jelly	Orange	Raspberry	Blackcurrant

Cartoons

It is best to beware of jokes and humour in illustrations for this can be a risky business. If you have ever given presentations to live audiences you will be aware that people's senses of humour can vary enormously. Jokes may fall flat, or people may miss the point. Worse still people might take offence. Cartoons are examples of humorous illustrations, and are the visual equivalent of the joke on paper. Using published cartoons is often very expensive but you may be talented in this yourself. Do think very carefully before using cartoons.

Decisions and Design

Be sure that your artwork is designed with the text and not added as an after thought – it almost always shows!

Decisions

It has been repeatedly stated that an illustration should complement text. It must add value – if you have any doubt about using an illustration do not do it! If you do decide to 'do it' remember that when glancing through a book or publication, it is the illustrations which catch the reader's eye. In those few minutes an impression can be made, which may be lasting.

If your illustrations need to be drawn professionally or re-drawn, your originals must be clear, noting any special measurements or other instructions for the artist. Always mark the required position for the artwork. Do not assume that someone will read through for the figure number and place the illustration close to it. Be explicit! Leave sufficient time for them to be returned to you for checking.

Design

The design of an illustration is very important. Do follow any advice from the publisher, journal editor, conference guidelines etc. An illustration can affect the balance of a page which is again why it should always be designed with the text and should always be located as close as possible to the relevant part.

To help readers understand your figure or graph, always make your visual big enough and bold enough to comprehend clearly. 'Keep the Illustration Simple' (KIS) and make sure it is not ambiguous. Any associated labelling should be in a good-sized print since small print can become obscured after reproduction. The

Figure 5.8: Portrait house

figure being an integral part of the text needs to be designed in the text, and not as an 'add-on'. The orientation i.e. vertical (portrait) or horizontal (landscape) of the illustration should also be considered.

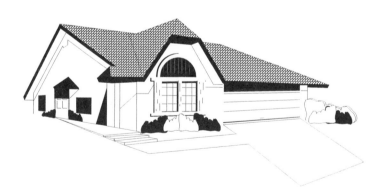

Figure 5.9: Landscape house

Unless extremely important or very complex, full-page sized illustrations should be avoided. If a full-page landscape illustration is to be used, the bottom should be at the right hand side of the page, otherwise the reader has to turn the book which is not conducive to easy reading! In such a case the page number would usually be omitted. Larger documents can take full-sized landscape illustrations but in a smaller-sized book, for example, this might be overpowering.

A logical numbering system should be part and parcel of your illustrations. You should decide initially what you are going to call your illustrations, for example, 'figures' or 'diagrams', and this frequently depends on your subject matter. You may wish to number figures according to chapter or section number in which case the numbering may appear as Figure 6.1, Figure 6.2 etc, meaning this is Figure 1 or 2 in Chapter 6.

A selection of numbering conventions is illustrated below:

Figure 1	Diagram 1.0
Figure 1.1	Diagram 1.1
Map A	Map I
Photo 1	Plate a
Photo 2	Plate b

Lettering

Most written work today is done using word-processing packages. Similarly any lettering associated with illustrations would probably use some type of software package. Having said this, some authors may wish to do their own lettering especially if it is a specialised script, for example, italic. However, be careful when selecting a type face to go with your illustration. Make sure that it is clear and legible. The size is also crucial. Too small and it will not reproduce well, too large and it will overpower the actual picture!

It is best to keep the same type face for captions or titles associated with your illustrations. This may or may not be the same as the written text. Be sure the font chosen is clear and easily legible.

Some clear styles to use are:

Times New Roman (Times New Roman)   Arial (Arial)

Garamond (Garamond)   Gill Sans (Gill Sans)

Avoid very fancy styles such as:

Mistral (*Mistral*)   Impact **(Impact)**

Haettenschweiler **(Haettenschweiler)**

Do not be tempted to use capital letters unless your illustration has a very short caption or title. Similarly lettering on the illustration should be kept to a minimum – it is after all a visual , too many words defeats the object.

Under my Thumb

Figure 5.10: Example of bad illustrations and lettering

   These figures are examples of bad illustrations and associated lettering. In Figure 5.10 the illustration is huge compared to the very small caption which seems to have been placed anywhere and without any numbering. In Figure 5.11 the reverse has occurred. The caption (again unnumbered) is enormous compared to the tiny visual of dominos.

DOMINO EFFECT

Figure 5.11: Example of bad illustrations and lettering

Preparing your Illustrations

Using words only to explain a floor plan or some type of numerical relationship is very difficult. In this instance an illustration will enhance understanding, and is precisely when an illustration ought to be used. Visual images can be used to inform, explain, instruct, educate, reinforce, but they can also annoy and confuse.

Good illustrations do not appear by chance. You do need to put thought into their purpose, appearance and learning objective. They must have congruence with the written word.

Here are six hints to follow when creating good illustrations:

(1)   Refer to the plan of your book or paper.
(2)   Sketch out your illustration (by hand or computerised).
(3)   Avoid over-detailing the illustration.
(4)   If you can use colour, make it pleasing to the eye. It can add emphasis and differentiate *but* beware of reds and green for the colour blind.
(5)   Make sure the print chosen is legible and conforms with guidelines.
(6)   Always double check the information on the illustration.

Captions

Captions are invaluable. It is essential that they are clear and understandable. They should contain all necessary information, yet avoid reproducing the text. Captions should not include any new information. They should describe the figure with a date and source where appropriate. These are usually placed in brackets. If the figure has been revised from the original, it should have 'after' within the brackets, for example,

Figure 8: An effective presentation (after Barnes, 1996)

Captions should be consistent throughout the text as should any conventions or symbols. Do not use any unnecessary wording in caption, for example, 'Map showing...'

The usual positioning of numbering and captions is flush left and below the figure or map. This positioning should also be consistent, and if you decide to centre captions or use some other positioning make sure this is adhered to throughout the publication.

Submission and Lists

Submission

Before submitting your paper it is helpful for the publisher to have text and illustrations separated. However *beware*, for this is where mistakes can easily happen. Therefore I suggest that you prepare illustrations very carefully in the following way:

(1)   List all illustrative material with illustration number and caption as they appear in the paper. For example in submitting this chapter, the figures would appear as:

> Figure 1: Illustrating
> Figure 2: 'Communication?'

(2)   Label all the artwork with figure, caption, author and paper title. You could create your own *proforma* for this, with boxes to tick. (See example opposite.)

(3)   Either place the labelled artwork in the order as it appears in the paper, as in (1), or collate illustrations of the same type together as their processing will be the same. Some publishers may request each individual item with instructions in a separate envelope.

(4)   Provide a separate list of captions.

(5)   Check each illustration carefully to ensure it is complete.

(6)   Mark the position of the illustration clearly in the text.

(7)   *Never* use a paper clip or staple artwork or write on the back of artwork.

(8)   Always keep a copy of the artwork you send to the publisher and copies of any lists or captions. These may be held as hard (paper) copy or on a computer's hard disk depending on how you work.

Lists

This can be one whole list of all types of 'Illustrations', unless separate numbering systems have been applied to maps, graphs , charts, tables etc., in which case separate lists need to be created. This will be required by the publisher and may also be used at the front of the book/paper if this is within the design specifications.

Illustration Proforma

TITLE:

AUTHOR:

Figure	☐	Table	☐	Map	☐
Graph	☐	Photo	☐	Diagram	☐
Chart	☐	Plate	☐	Flow Chart	☐

Number:

Caption:

Chapter/Section:

•   Any Special Instructions:

•   Comments from Publisher:

Illustration 'CHECKLIST'

In the rush to write a useful and interesting paper the artwork may well be one aspect that is not given a great deal of time. All through this chapter the point has been made that any visuals should complement the text and be an integral part of it. Look therefore at the checklist below (which will not take a long time) and then you will be sure that any illustrations you use will be worthwhile and appreciated by the reader.

Before creating an illustration and certainly before submission to an editor or conference, it may be useful to use the following checklist:

- Is it appropriate?
- Is it clear?
- Is it relevant?
- Have you labelled correctly?
- Is it complete?
- Is it the best type of visual?
- Does it show what you want it to show?
- Have you marked the position of the illustrations?
- Have you given any special instructions to publisher?
- Have you sought permissions from source?
- Have you received (or paid) copyright clearance?
- Have you checked them before publication?

By using the tips suggested in this chapter you should be able to illustrate any academic work to a high standard with relevant and informative visuals. There are many more ideas and tips and no doubt you will have your own ideas on the way your work should look. This chapter merely gives some rhyme, reason and ideas on good illustrations which, it is hoped, you will find useful.

> Remember it is up to you to make your illustration worth a thousand words!

References

Achtert, J.G.W. (1977) *MLA Handbook for Writers of Research Papers*. New York: The Modern Language Association of America.

Butcher, J. (1992) *Copy-editing*. Cambridge: Cambridge University Press.

Carrol, L. (1865) *Alice's Adventures in Wonderland*. London: Macmillan.

Ericson, J. (1987) *Publish or Perish*. (1st edn) Ely: Peter Francis Publishers.

Hill, M. and Cochran, W. (1977) *Into Print*. California: William Kaufmann.

Nankivell, C. and Shoolbred, M. (1995) *Presenting Information*. London: The Library Association.

Wells, G. (1981) *The Successful Authors Handbook*. London: Macmillan.

(Sources for illustrations and maps are reproduced from Microsoft Clip Art.)

Chapter 6

Proof-reading and Correction

by Nancy Harrison

WHEN you submit your paper to a journal it will be in one of two forms: hard copy or electronic files. The latter will be sent to an editor on a disk or as an e-mail. At present most paper-based journals require both hard copy and a disk when you submit the final version of your paper. A fully electronic journal may only need your files sent as an e-mail. Here we shall be concerned with paper-based journals as you will receive a copy of the page proofs for correction when your paper is set prior to publication.

It is necessary to think about proof-correction at the point of submitting your original manuscript; you cannot expect editors or typesetters to be mind-readers. The term 'manuscript' is a general term referring to the material that is in your article, thesis, essay or contribution; when we refer to' hard copy ', that is the material printed on paper. You may wonder why we talk about proof reading hard copy when many personal computers allow you to edit *on screen*. The ability to change words and shift text round is useful but to find and correct mistakes there is no substitute for seeing the words actually printed on paper, whether by a typewriter or an electronic printer. You should always proof-read hard copy. If you send in something full of spelling mistakes and grammatical errors, badly laid out, with illegible corrections and many afterthoughts, you can look forward to trouble at the proof stage.

However sophisticated your software may be, for proof checking nothing beats the human eye. Do not rely blindly on spelling checkers; they can be both bossy and ignorant. Mine once refused to use the word 'supererogatory', which has a specific meaning, and insisted on substituting the word 'superiority' which was nonsensical in the context. I had to recast the sentence to resolve the deadlock. Spelling checkers are only as good as the vocabulary they contain, which often leaves a lot to be desired. Make sure that the one you rely on has no American spelling, for example.

Follow the "Notes for Authors" supplied by the journal and obey all the instructions they give you. You will need, for example, to supply details of the software that you used to generate the electronic files together with the names of the files.

Typesetting will be carried out from a disk if one has been supplied so it is essential that the hard copy and disk are identical. If you have made no mistakes in the disk version, theoretically there should be no errors in the proofs when you receive them. However, many strange things can happen in the process of converting the electronic version to the paper version. Gremlins can get in and make changes you did not intend. A recent example was a paper where all occurrences of the word 'quantitative' had turned into 'qualitative', a disaster for the author's quantitative study!

Formatting can also change when your electronic version is altered to the one used by the typesetter. Human errors can creep in at this point. For example, an editor with little or no knowledge of your subject area can change the meaning of your work by well-intentioned alteration of your punctuation.

Proof-reading

At last the printed copy has come to you, and you begin to search for errors as a thrush hunts for worms. But it is very difficult to spot small errors in your own work. You know what you wanted to say and that is what your mind sees on the paper rather than the misspelt word or the lack of an essential comma.

First you must check all the headings, then read through each page slowly. If you read it aloud you are more likely to spot mistakes. To pick up the literals and punctuation errors, try reading, finally, line by line from the bottom of the page to the top. If you meticulously mark your own copy of the manuscript with the same markings that were on the copy that went to the printer, you will be able to distinguish those mistakes which are the printer's responsibility from those which were due to your own oversight or carelessness. The usual convention is for printer's errors to be marked in red; yours are in blue. Try to aim at a majority of red marks.

Remember that the printer does not give a hoot about the content of your work. To the printer, a classic work on philosophy, a mathematical treatise, a magazine article and a bad poem are equal. He is there to print what you want. What you write may be gibberish, but it will be printed all the same. The printer's business is to reproduce accurately what is in the manuscript.

There is a difference, however, in the way in which the proofs are regarded. In setting from the manuscript, each word in each line will be read. When corrected proofs are read, the printer will note only what is in the margin of each page. It is essential that every correction you make in the text must be given the right marginal mark next to the line.

Do not invent your own marks or write out corrections. Use the British Standard proof correction symbols. If the error is large or too complex to be dealt with by the accepted marks, write in the correction at the foot of the page or the top and circle it round, leading up to an arrow pointing out the place where the correction must be made.

Sometimes a whole paragraph or a couple of lines are left out. The marginal mark is 'out see copy', with a mark in the text to show where the omission occurred. It is important that when this has happened you send the relevant part of the text back with the proofs so that the printer can see what should have been there.

The way to deal with some errors may not be obvious from the list of standard marks. One little problem that can crop up is the badly broken word, where the printer has come to the end of the line and has had to split a word. The break should never confuse the reader. Words beginning with 'ex' should never be broken at that point. The ex-ample must be shown as examp-le, not as exam-ple. Read-just is bad; re-adjust is good. Ar-mour is better than arm-our. If you discover a bad break, the marginal mark is 'take over' if you want letters to be transferred to the next line or 'take back' if you feel they should go in the line above.

If a word is hyphenated and you have the misfortune to find that the hyphen ends a line in your manuscript, you should put three little dots under the hyphen and 'stet' in the margin. If the printer has overlooked your mark or you forgot to draw attention to the hyphen, when you are correcting the proofs make a mark in the text at the end of the line and put 'stet hyphen' in the margin.

In proof-correcting you may use both left and right margins. If there are many corrections in a single line it is less confusing to use the margins on either side. Do try to keep the marks clear and unambiguous and be sure that the mark is beside the right line. The printer will hate you if a search has to be made for the right place in the text.

As an exercise on page 83 you will find an example of a manuscript which you can photocopy and then mark up the corrections, using the proof correction symbols which follow. Then compare it with the marked sheet on page 84. Page 85 shows the example after it has been corrected by the printer.

Extracts from BS 5261: Part 2: 1976 (1991) are reproduced with the permission of BSI under licence no. PD\1998 1798. Complete editions of the standards can be obtained by post from BSI Customer Services, 389 Chiswick High Road, London W4 4AL.

Marks for copy preparation and proof correction

Instruction	Textual mark	Marginal mark
Insert in text the matter indicated in the margin	⋏	New matter followed by ⋏
Substitute character or words	/ through character or ⊢——⊣ through word(s)	New character or new word(s)
Insert additional material identified by a letter in a diamond	⋏	⋏ Followed by for example ◈
Delete and close up	⸮ through character(s) or ⊏⊐	⸮
Set in or change to capital letters	≡≡≡ under character(s)	≡≡≡
Change capital letters to lower-case letters	Encircle character(s) to be changed	≠
Close up to normal inter-line spacing	(each side of column)	
Insert space between lines or paragraphs	⊐— or —⊏	Give the amount of space when necessary
Indent	⊏	⌐ Give the amount of ⌊ the indent
Transpose characters or words	⎍⎀ between characters or words	⎍⎀

Photocopy this example and mark it.

in as few wrds as possible and arrange what you have written in one or two paragraphs. Only now need you start to count words and edit what you have written. Lamb's essay A Chapter on ears can be reduced to one paragraph:

First draft:

The writer says he has no ears. This is not meant in the physical sense: he has no ear for music. He is also tone deaf and so finds concerts and professional performances, particularly concertos,

painful and depressing. He is unusually susceptible to noise, even that of a carpenter's hammer. When he was was young and sentimental he enjoyed hearing a WOMAN sing, accompanying herself on the harpsichord. His friend Nov ... holds parties at which he plays the organ. Lamb enjoys the music at first but finds too much of it overwhelming. He is glad when supper is served.

Second ddaft:

Lamb claims to have no ear for music. He is tone-deaf, finding music played at concerts meaningless, painful and depressing, being distressed by noise of any kind. As a sentimental youth he enjoyed hearing a woman paly the harpsichord and sing, but when his friend Nov..., playijg the organ, goes on too long, pleasure turns to oppression and he welcomes the arrival of supper.

The original, Lamb's essay, is much better and full of humour. It also takes up five pages.

Check your marks with the ones below.

in as few words as possible and arrange what you have written in one or two paragraphs. Only now need you start to count words and edit what you have written. Lamb's essay/A Chapter on ears/can be reduced to one paragraph:

First draft:

The writer says he has no ears. This is not meant in the physical sense: he has no ear for music. He is also tone deaf and so finds concerts and professional performances, particularly concertos,

painful and depressing. He is unusually susceptible to noise, even that of a carpenter's hammer. When he was (was) young and sentimental he enjoyed hearing a WOMAN sing, accompanying herself on the harpsichord. His friend Nov … holds parties at which he plays the organ. Lamb enjoys the music at first but finds too much of it overwhelming. He is glad when supper is served.

Second draft:

Lamb claims to have no ear for music. He is tone-deaf, finding music played at concerts meaningless, painful and depressing, being distressed by noise of any kind. As a sentimental youth he enjoyed hearing a woman play the harpsichord and sing, but when his friend Nov…, playing the organ, goes on too long, pleasure turns to oppression and he welcomes the arrival of supper.

The original, Lamb's essay, is much better and full of humour. It also takes up five pages.

to his guests

Here is the corrected example.

in as few words as possible and arrange what you have written in one or two paragraphs. Only now need you start to count words and edit what you have written. Lamb's essay, "A Chapter on Ears", can be reduced to one paragraph:

First draft:

> The writer says he has no ears. This is not meant in the physical sense; he has no ear for music. He is also tone deaf and so finds concerts and professional performances, particularly concertos, painful and depressing. He is unusually susceptible to noise, even that of a carpenter's hammer. When he was young and sentimental he enjoyed hearing a woman sing, accompanying herself on the harpsichord. His friend Nov ... holds parties at which he plays the organ. Lamb enjoys the music at first but finds too much of it overwhelming. He is glad when supper is served.

Second draft:

> Lamb claims to have no ear for music. He is tone-deaf, finding music played at concerts meaningless, painful and depressing, being distressed by noise of any kind. As a sentimental youth he enjoyed hearing a woman play the harpsichord and sing, but when his friend Nov ..., playing the organ to his guests, goes on too long, pleasure turns to oppression and he welcomes the arrival of supper.

The original, Lamb's essay, is much better and full of humour. It also takes up five pages.

Do practice proof-reading. This is easily done. When the electronic revolution overtook the newspapers, reporters began to send in their stories directly from their laptops. The stories were then electronically set without the intervention of a sub-editor and it was soon apparent that many reporters on even the upmarket papers could not spell and had a shaky knowledge of grammar and syntax. So use your morning paper as an exercise and mark up mistakes; you should find enough to work on!

Chapter 7

Copyright

by Allison Coleman

Importance of Copyright

*F*OR the general public and the average academic, copyright law has come
into much greater prominence in the last few years. We have become an
information rich society. It is much easier to copy materials for use in private
research, teaching, the production of distance learning packs, study packs,
multi-media packages, pages on the Internet etc.; and copying and recycling
has been encouraged by increased class size, educational trends, fashion,
teaching quality assessments and the pressure to publish. This has brought to
the fore the clash of interests between, on the one hand, the users who want
free and unfettered use of copyright materials and, on the other hand, the
owners and creators who object to plagiarism and free-rider behaviour and
who claim a just reward for their efforts and skill.

The free-use argument of the users has become louder as the costs of
access to electronic information and the costs of copying have decreased.
Why, they argue, should we not use the materials which we have photocopied
and/or downloaded and distribute them freely to others, particularly if those
others have limited financial resources? Who will find out? Is it not quicker to
compile the work of others than to write everything afresh? Yet, would the
producer of such materials happily see others copy and use those works either
without payment or without attribution, especially if he or she was not a
salaried employee and was dependent on royalty income to earn a living? In
countries where illegal copying is endemic, copyright industries such as
publishing, sound recording, software houses and film distribution cannot
survive with consequent damage to employment and indigenous culture. It is

not however the function of this chapter to debate the morality of copyright, but the law must be seen against the stresses and strains of the system. The following account should enable an author subject to demands to publish or perish to operate legitimately when copying and using the materials of others and to protect his or her own work when there is improper use of it by others.

An author needs to be aware of the following copyright issues:

(1)   Who owns copyright in the new work?

- Does it belong to him or her?
- Does it belong to his or her employer?
- Does the publisher require an assignment of copyright under the publishing agreement and if so can or should the author object?

(2)   What is protected by copyright?

(3)   What are the rights of others whose works might be used in the process of writing the new work, for example, poems, maps and tables etc. created by others and relied on, quoted from or otherwise incorporated into the new work?

- Who owns copyright in the other work?
- How long does copyright last?
- To whom does it pass on death and how do you trace the heirs?
- What happens if a publisher which owns copyright has gone out of business?
- To what extent may the works of others be used or quoted from legitimately?
- What degree of free use does the law allow and what has to be paid for?
- Can permission to use be refused?

These are some of the issues which will be addressed in this chapter. However a warning must be issued that the law of copyright is complex, riddled with exceptions and changes with the date and type of work. When in doubt, consult an expert. The references at the end of the chapter may also be of use.

Sources of the Law

The most recent statute is the Copyright, Designs and Patents Act 1988 (the 1988 Act) which governs works created after 1st August 1989. However, previous Copyright Acts are still important and may apply to works created before that date. The 1988 Act applies only to the United Kingdom. Different laws apply in other countries, but there has been substantial international harmonisation of principles to ensure copyright protection in other countries, not just in the country of origin of the author or the work. This is very important as the market for many copyright works is global.

What Rights does Copyright Confer?

Copyright confers two main sets of rights: economic rights and moral rights. Economic rights enable a copyright owner to earn money. They are the exclusive rights to do any of the following six acts:

(1)   to copy the work;
(2)   to issue copies to the public;
(3)   to lend or rent the work to the public;
(4)   to perform, play or show the work in public;
(5)   to broadcast the work or include it in a cable programme;
(6)   to make an adaptation of the work or to do any of the above with an adaptation.

Because the rights are exclusive to the owner of copyright, he or she is the only person entitled to do any of the acts listed above; others need the consent of the copyright owner and consent can be conditional on payment of a fee. There is no statutory control on the level of the fee, and consent may be refused.

Doing an act without the permission of the copyright owner amounts to infringement of copyright. Note however that certain things are allowed under the 1988 Act. These are known as permitted acts. The one most frequently relied on by academics doing their research and by students is 'fair dealing for the purposes of research or private study'. This legitimises photocopying of a certain proportion of a copyright work. Authors when writing a piece rely mainly on the provisions relating to criticism and review. Infringement of copyright and permitted acts are considered further below.

The author of a work also has moral rights. These are

(1)   the right to be identified as the author of a work;
(2)   the right to object to derogatory treatment;
(3)   the right to object to false attribution; and
(4)   the right to privacy of certain films and photographs.

Moral rights have become particularly useful to authors whose works are published electronically, then reproduced in whole or in part without being correctly attributed, or which have been copied from a database or the Internet, then published in an altered form.

Moral rights were granted only grudgingly by the British government in the 1988 Act. They are hedged by complications. Good practice requires their observance, but the law sometimes takes them away. The best general advice is when using the materials of others, observe moral rights; and when writing, always insist that a book contract contains a clause that the rights of the author are asserted under the 1988 Act, or simply that 'All rights are reserved'. Moral rights remain the property of the author and cannot be assigned to a publisher.

One important limitation on copyright is that it protects only the way in which material is set out, that is, its expression, it does not protect the underlying idea. So long as a work is not actually copied, either wholly or substantially, lifting the underlying idea and expressing it in a different way amounts only to plagiarism. Plagiarism is a transgression of academic good practice and may breach disciplinary rules but it does not necessarily involve breach of copyright.

Copyright also does not protect against independent creation. If two people independently create identical works, both are protected by copyright and neither infringes the copyright of the other. However, the more complex the work, the less the likelihood of independent creation and the greater the chance of copying, whether consciously or unconsciously.

What is Protected by Copyright Laws?

Copyright law protects nine main categories of what are known as works:

- original literary, dramatic, musical or artistic works;
- sound recordings, films, broadcasts or cable programmes; and
- the typographical arrangement of published editions.

Many of these categories are subdivided. Literary works, for instance, covers 'a table or compilation and ... a computer program', thus protecting football pools, anthologies of poems and software packages; an artistic work means, amongst other things, 'a graphic work, photograph, sculpture or collage'; and 'graphic work' is further defined as including a painting, drawing, diagram, map, chart or plan, engraving, etching, lithograph, woodcut or similar work.

Ownership of a physical item does not imply ownership of copyright in it. The purchaser of a compact disc of a Lloyd Weber musical does not obtain copyright in the music and lyrics and does not have the right to copy it without permission. The purchaser of a painting cannot sell Christmas cards reproducing the painting without the consent of the owner of copyright in the painting.

Who Owns Copyright?

Sections 9 to 11 of the Copyright, Designs and Patents Act 1988 provide that the author of a work is the first owner of copyright in it, and that the author of a work is the person who creates it. Where a work is created by two or more authors in circumstances where the contribution of each is not distinct from that of the others, the work is known as a work of joint authorship and all of the authors are collectively the owners of copyright in the work.

One important exception is section 11 of the 1988 Act which provides that where a literary, dramatic, musical or artistic work is made by an employee in the course of employment, the employer is the first owner of any copyright in the work, subject to any agreement to the contrary. This section does not apply to consultants. They therefore retain copyright in works created by them unless they agree in writing to transfer copyright to another.

Section 11 can be varied by contract. Many academic institutions have agreements with their employees that they will not assert their right to copyright. In that case, the academic retains copyright as the author of the work. This waiver by the university or college protects academic freedom in that if the university had copyright it could refuse permission to publish. There have been calls for universities to reclaim copyright to counteract the power of the publishers, but these should be resisted, otherwise academic freedom may be seriously undermined.

Assignments and Licensing

The first time an author contemplates copyright is often when faced with a publishing contract which contains a clause requiring the author to assign copyright to the publisher. The author may do this only if, of course, he or she owns copyright, that is, if section 11 does not apply and copyright does not belong to the employer. If it belongs to the employer only a duly authorised person may assign.

An assignment of copyright must be in writing. It may be of the full copyright or be limited in time (for example, for five years) or subject matter (paperback rights only). An assignment should be contrasted with a copyright licence. An assignment transfers ownership, whereas a licence gives the licensee more limited rights, usually, in this context the right to publish, and that right may be exclusive or non-exclusive. A licence does not transfer ownership in the copyright which therefore remains with the author or employer.

Assigning copyright can cause problems for an author. The most common one is that the work cannot be published elsewhere without the permission of the assignee (the person to whom it has been assigned). The author may not contemplate re-publication directly, but once established in a field, he or she may be asked to write on a topic many times. It is difficult not to use the same style, structure, sequence and organisation, particularly if a subject matter is best presented in a certain way, and copyright (which is now owned by another) can be infringed by the original author not only by word for word reproduction, but also by copying a substantial part. The use of the word-processor increases the inclination to re-use or to borrow substantially, but this must be avoided if a licence to re-use has not been obtained. In practice however, publishers are quite reasonable when it comes to re-working, so long as the new work does not detract from sales of the old.

One advantage of an assignment of copyright to a publisher is that the publisher, as copyright owner, has the right to sue any infringer of copyright. Books are often pirated in other countries and a lone author is unlikely to know of the infringement and even less likely to have the time, resources or inclination to sue, whereas the publishers frequently take action to enforce their rights. However this advantage can also be conferred by licence. On balance an author is probably in a better position if he or she grants a copyright licence to a publisher rather than assigning copyright, but in most instances the publishers, particularly of academic works, have greater bargaining power and authors have little choice but to agree.

Care should be taken when a contract requires an author both to assign copyright and to agree to keep confidential information concerning the project. This combination is often found in government research contracts. It allows the government to prevent publication (using the copyright clause) and to prevent disclosure of the results (using the confidentiality clause) if it does not approve the results of the research.

Copyright and Death or Dissolution of a Business

On the death of an author, copyright passes under the will of the author, or to the next of kin on an intestacy. (A person dies intestate if there is no will or partially intestate if the will does not cover the item concerned). If the work is unpublished and there are no contrary provisions in the will, a gift of the original document or other material embodying the copyright work (for example, a painting) will pass copyright to the donee as well as physical ownership of the thing. If an author becomes bankrupt, copyright passes to the trustee in bankruptcy and is then disposed of in accordance with the laws of bankruptcy (for persons) or insolvency (for companies).

Problems can arise when a firm which owns copyright goes out of business. If the firm is a company which becomes insolvent, copyright passes to the trustee in bankruptcy who will then sell copyright along with the other assets of the business. If the company is taken over, copyright will normally pass to the new owner. If a partnership is dissolved, property will pass under the terms of the dissolution contract. If there is none, it will remain in the joint ownership of the partners, this time in their capacity as individuals. However, many firms just go out of business without any legal formalities being observed. There then may be no owner of copyright or, to put it another way, there may be no-one to sue for infringement. For all practical purposes copyright then falls into the public domain and anyone may use the materials. This is fine for users of copyright works, but not an ideal solution for authors who have for example assigned copyright to publishers and who wish to control the use of their works. There is no automatic reverter of copyright to the author following an assignment unless an express clause to this effect has been incorporated in the publishing agreement. This is therefore another matter to check in the pre-contractual stage. An author who has merely licensed copyright is in a much better position, for here the licensing agreement will come to an end, and the author, as owner, will be free to exploit and protect the copyright material.

Duration of Copyright

Under the Copyright, Designs and Patents Act 1988 copyright in literary, dramatic, musical and artistic works lasted for the life of the author, plus fifty years. Since 1st January 1996, the copyright term for most of these works has been extended by the Duration of Copyright Regulations 1995 (the 1995 Regulations) to life plus seventy years. This means that many works which had dropped out of copyright are now once again protected by what is known as 'revived copyright'. The 1995 Regulations are exceptionally complicated and are generally beyond the scope of this chapter. A useful account can be found in Flint (1997: 45-65) where he reproduces a table by John Adams and Michael Edenborough which details the changes. This can also be found, with explanatory text, in Adams and Edenborough (1996) work. However, even they, two of the leading copyright lawyers, state that they cannot guarantee that they have not made any mistakes, such is the complexity of the law. Reform along these lines in frankly ridiculous.

The rights of copyright owners in works protected by revived copyright have been reduced. Anyone can do what they like with a work providing that they pay a reasonable royalty or other remuneration to the copyright owner. If the parties fail to agree, the payment will be determined by the Copyright Tribunal. However in order to take advantage of this improved position the user of the work must give reasonable notice to the copyright owner of his intention to use the work. If notice is given, the acts will be deemed to have been licensed even though the rate of payment may not be agreed before publication. It will still therefore be necessary to search for the copyright owner before publication, as with other copyright materials. The owner of revived copyright is the person who was the owner of copyright immediately before it would have expired under the old law. These rules do not apply to works which have their copyrights extended automatically to life plus seventy years, only to those which have fallen out of copyright, then been revived. Where there has been no interruption of the copyright term, the normal rules apply and permission to use can be refused.

Infringement of Copyright

There are two types of infringement or breach of copyright: primary and secondary. Primary infringement involves breach only of the civil rights of the copyright owner; and it can be committed innocently, that is, there is no need for the infringer to know that the work is protected by copyright, or that the act constitutes infringement. Primary infringement is not a criminal offence (*cf* secondary infringement, below).

As stated above, an owner of copyright has the exclusive right to do any of the following six acts. If anyone else does any of these acts without permission, it will amount to primary infringement of copyright. They are

(1)   in relation to all categories of work, to copy the work (section 17 of the 1988 Act);

(2)   in relation to all categories of work, to issue copies to the public (section 18);

(3)   to rent or lend the work to the public (section 18A);

(4)   in relation to literary, dramatic and musical works, to perform the work in public; and, in relation to sound recordings, films, broadcasts and cable programmes, to play or show the work in public (section 19);

(5)   in relation to all works except typographical arrangements, to broadcast the work or include it in a cable programme (section 20);

(6)   in relation to a literary, dramatic and musical work, to make an adaptation of the work, or to do any of the acts listed in (1) to (5) with an adaptation (section 21).

The whole work need not be copied, performed etc. so long as a substantial part is used without consent. Copying a section of a work can therefore breach copyright. The test as to whether a part is substantial is not just related to the quantity of what is taken, but also takes into account its quality – is it an important part, or key component, or a clearly recognisable part? If it is qualitatively important, it does not matter that the part taken is in fact quite small in relation to the work as a whole. To some extent the courts work on the principle that if it is worth taking, it must be important and is worth protecting by copyright. This means that the copier has to be very careful. There are no hard and fast rules. If in doubt, seek permission.

The remedies for primary infringement of copyright are an injunction to prevent further breach of the law, or damages for a breach which has already occurred. There are also very useful procedures for search of premises and seizure of infringing items or the means for making them, such as the copying machines, computers etc. It should however be noted that certain acts will not amount to infringement of copyright. These exceptions are discussed below under the heading of permitted acts.

Secondary infringement of copyright breaches the civil rights of the copyright owner, but is also a criminal offence. Basically it involves dealing in copyright works; or providing the means for making infringing copies; or permitting or enabling a public performance to take place in breach of copyright. However in order to be liable the infringer must have a 'guilty mind', that is, must know or have reason to believe that there is a breach of copyright.

The penalties for secondary infringement are quite severe.

Permitted Acts

Researchers rely heavily on one particular exception to copyright protection. This is what is called 'fair dealing' for the purposes of research or private study and it enables students and researchers to copy (for example, photocopy) a proportion of a literary, dramatic, musical or artistic work (but note, not the other works such as sound recordings) without infringing copyright in it, or, in the case of a published edition, without infringing copyright in the typographical arrangement (which belongs to the publisher).

The governing principle in this particular provision is that the copying must be fair. In the United States, it is known as 'the fair use provision', a description which is arguably better than our notion of fair dealing. If the copying is of a large proportion of a work which is in print and available in the bookshops, the use will invariably be unfair and the copying will breach copyright.

Assessing fairness can obviously be quite difficult. Publishers have reached agreements called licensing agreements with universities and others which set out what in their view is fair use. Persons who copy within these guidelines will not be sued for infringement of copyright, nor will their employers. The full text of these licensing agreements is held by the institution, but it is found in summary form alongside most photocopying machines. However, licensing agreements and practice notes issued by organisations are not statements of law, they only represent the views of the parties as to what is fair dealing. The courts may take a different view. Employees who flout the law do however not merely subject themselves to the possibility of litigation, but also their employers. Most academic institutions are keen not to face the possibility or publicity of a law suit. This is why they enter into licensing agreements and employees who breach them may face disciplinary proceedings.

Authors in their writings make frequent reference to the works of others. If the ideas of another are used, but not the expression of the other, there can be no breach of copyright, for, as we saw above, copyright protects the form in which a work is set out and not the underlying ideas as such. The other author should however be adequately referenced to avoid allegations of plagiarism, rather than breach of copyright laws.

If an author wishes to quote from the work of another, or use maps, drawings or tables of another, copyright may be infringed unless the act is permitted under another heading, namely, fair dealing for the purposes of criticism or review. The criticism or review may be of the work itself, or of a performance of it, and in both cases it must accompanied by a sufficient acknowledgement. Again the governing principle is that the use (or dealing) must be fair. Sufficient acknowledgement is to some extent governed by custom and practice, but if there is any doubt the more fulsome the reference the better.

Various other acts are permitted by the 1988 Act in the sense that performing any one of these acts will not amount to breach of copyright. They relate mainly to copying by libraries and copying for the purposes of educational instruction. However this chapter concentrates on the plight of the author who must publish or perish rather than the teacher who needs to prepare materials for pure teaching purposes. They are therefore omitted and other works on copyright law should be consulted.

References

Adams, J. and Edenborough, M. (1996) "The Duration of Copyright in the United Kingdom after the 1995 Regulations", *EIPR*, 11.

Copinger and Skone James (1998) *Copyright*. (14th edn, K. Garnett, ed.) London: Sweet and Maxwell.

Flint (1997) *A User's Guide to Copyright*. (4th edn) London: Butterworth.

Laddie, H., Prescott and Vittoria, M. (1995) *The Modern Law of Copyright*. (2nd edn) London: Butterworth.

Post, J.B. and Foster, M.R. (1992) *Copyright – A Handbook for Archivists*. London: The Society for Archivists.

Chapter 8

'Living on the Front Line': stresses and strains on academic editors

by Chris Rowley

Introduction

AT one time academic journal editorship was viewed by many as a mysterious, but nevertheless worthy, position and occupation for those in academia to aspire to. Reaching such 'lofty' heights as becoming a journal editor was seen, and taken, almost as a sign of achievement and prominence in academia. Departments liked to bask in the reflected glory from any of their members actually engaged in such editorship. Indeed, editorship, common anecdotal evidence would have us believe, was one of those collection of 'tasks' needed to help in the construction of an academic's comprehensive CV and useful for career progression. The output of this editorship was the publication of journals that were often weighty tombs frequently filled with scholarly, well-written work. These journals accumulated, were stacked on library shelves in ever-lengthening runs and some of their contents referred to over and over again *en route* to becoming 'classics' of a minor or even major nature. Many of the journal entries went on to gain the well-thumbed look and feel, almost falling open at the most 'required' pages when turned to by a fresh reader.

This rough and ready picture, some might say, is more of a caricature. It certainly seems an increasingly less accurate and partial portrayal of an editor's lot than it used to be. However, what many of us will probably not disagree about is that there have been myriad changes in the education and publication sectors which have made impacts on many aspects of academic editorship. These stem from several simultaneous pressures, the results of which on editorship often remain unseen or unregistered by other actors in the publication process chain. The causes and impacts of these pressures may be debated, and this forms the core of this piece, whose structure is as follows. The contextual changes afflicting academic journal editors are outlined. These can roughly be divided into both 'push' and 'pull' factors increasing the volume, velocity and variability of submissions to many academic journal editors. The main results of pressures on editors, including their paradoxical nature, is the focus of the next section. Some key conclusions for editors are then outlined.

Contextual Changes

What has caused these multiple changes to editorial work? These shifts can be roughly divided into twin pressures, both input and output related, seemingly exacerbated, in the late 1980s and early 1990s.

Push Factors

On one hand there were 'push' factors increasing the 'in-flow' to editors of communications and enquiries concerning possible, and actually submitted, papers to be considered for publication in journals. Some contributors began keeping ever closer and parental tabs on their paper's progress along the uneven and often rocky road of the publication process. This in itself escalated the stresses and strains on editors.

The increase in the volume of submissions was the result of several developments. There could be the simple quantitative expansion of academia and so, all other things being equal, we may well have expected more submissions for the more 'traditional' reasons for publishing, including reporting key findings and developing subjects and theories, feelings of satisfaction, egos, career progression, and so on.

However, as most of us are all too fully aware, the real driver of this mushrooming of papers was the massively increased pressure on academics to 'publish or perish', particularly in journals, and especially in refereed journals. This stems from the ubiquitously and tiredly talked about 'research assessment exercises'. Such publications are now taken as a proxy 'macho' measure of 'research activeness' in these exercises and inter-institutional comparisons of 'worth'. These assessments are not one-off events, but ongoing and repeated processes. It often makes one feel that these are leaving in their wake a trail of publications that are no longer 'important' (for these narrow purposes at least), and so seemingly 'disregarded'.

Universities, departments and 'line managers' have had to react to these stimuli as Pavlov's dogs. We can all think of examples of the crude 'stick approach' being attempted to force some (sometimes initially bewildered and shocked) colleagues into becoming reluctant researchers and to publish prevalently and continuously. The threat involved in this procedure is often the possible severe 'sentence' of being sent to the 'gulags' of increasingly mass teaching and administration of what are frequently perceived as poorer and poorer quality students (even, as is now being increasingly admitted, in the 'old' universities). Yet, this 'stick' is made more brittle and less persuasive when the bearers of often crudely relayed tidings are academics over-promoted into managerial roles on the basis of research and publication track records. They have frequently not obtained their positions on the basis of their accumulation of, or knowledge about, even basic skills in the areas of motivation or 'man-management' (this term is used in a non-gender specific way). The result of these trends and developments is, as the lyrics go, 'an accident waiting to happen': in short, demotivation, jealousy, turnover and conflicts.

The folly and very corrosive nature of these repeated publication-led exercises is too easily brushed aside or even not registered. Notions of academic 'community', collegiality and mutual-help are being increasingly undermined. This erosion has occurred at the macro, inter-institutional level. After all, 'league tables' are constructed to display graphically 'rankings'. In turn, these (given the fixed nature of a 'pot' of research funding), imply that institutions are engaged in a competitive, zero-sum game. A similarly invidious process at the micro level can be seen in departments, as individuals become labelled as either research 'active' or 'non-active', and their work patterns, demands put on them and conditions, all commensurately and increasingly diverge. Are there no 'shades of grey' here I often wonder? Is this labelling to be a one-off event? Indicatively, the very use of such value-laded and polar opposite 'either/or' terms as 'active', with its positive connotations, and 'non-active', giving the impression of dormancy and the person being a 'slacker', is problematic. These have become normative. Also, the mechanisms used to reach these judgements and labels of 'active' versus 'non-active' researchers are not based on some 'objective' or 'pseudo-scientific' measure. They are sometimes arbitrarily and subjectively measured or, even worse, underpinned by political or personal reasons. The resentment of those (ex)-colleagues increasingly 'ghettoized' into teaching but still comparing themselves with those labelled and lauded as 'key researchers' that 'need to be protected', is all too obvious. We should not forget that research is undertaken and published by not just those institutionally and officially actually labelled 'researchers', but also by those employed under the rubric of 'lecturer', and its connotations of teaching, student contact, administration, and even pastoral duties, and so on. All these developments are exacerbated in the contemporary education sector, with institutions seen as businesses, with revenue streams, and naïve notions of 'marketisation' and culture of 'customer care'. These partly imply explicit, external methods of performance measures of teaching quality in a more evaluative manner, such as appraisals and links to perform-ance 'indicators', such as student assessments, teaching quality audits, and so on. Are they then used in a constructive, developmental manner and frame-work? Or, are they simply another managerial tool in its armoury to be used against you?

What do institutions and management actually think goes through people's minds in these sorts of situations? It is simply not good enough for them to use the rhetorical sop that both teaching and research are work of equal value and worth, especially when it comes to career enhancement and promotion. I am sure many of us have been involved in all too many recruitment processes that expose the shallowness of these platitudes. Too often rankings of an individual's worth is made by defaulting to crude criteria based on personal 'inputs' (research grants gained, and especially current, and where from) and 'outputs' (number of articles, especially submissible for the next assessment exercise, in what they consider to be the 'top' refereed journals). As an aside, the gaining of these research grants again can be at the cost of teaching, particularly as the two spheres are not explicitly linked in applications.

Too many academics do not seem to see that not all institutions, depart-ments and individuals can be 'winners' in this latest 'game'. Can every university, department and academic be actively researching and publishing, be 'world class' and have an 'international reputation'? I think not. Is it help-ful for departments to be de-stabilised by the 'merry-go-round' of poaching and replacing of 'star publishers', a process that escalates up as the next assessment exercise approaches to get people *in situ* before the 'music stops'? Many assessments are simply political exercises and self-fulfilling prophesies trying to maintain the *status quo* after the removal of the old binary divide in education. There are, obviously, limits to so-called 'productivity' from academics: they can only reduce exposure to students, teaching and admin-istration, while simultaneously boosting funding applications, research and publications to a certain, finite level. This simple truth is now somewhat too easily forgotten or ignored.

Pull Factors

On the other hand, there are also pervasive 'pull' factors on the increasing volume of papers submitted and also on individual editors' workloads, demands and stresses. These come from pressures from the publishers of the journals themselves. This is due to an inter-locking mix of technological, ownership and organisational changes in the industry. The publishing sector has seen some consolidation, with mergers, acquisitions and takeovers. It has become, it is frequently argued, more 'competitive' and so requiring more 'professional' management. Yet, this is often simply translated into the search for greater profits in the short term; that is, it is often sought out through squeezing labour content by removing employees and forcing those who are left to work harder and more intensively or displacing all manner of work onto 'non-employees'. There has certainly been a publishing technological revolution, with a large and continuing decline in publication costs of production and reduction of entry barriers into the industry. This has in turn put pressure on 'traditional' publishers to adapt, to fight back with reductions in their own costs and workforces.

Allied to this trend has been a common search for ever larger economies of scale by publishers: why run just a couple of journals when you can have many more in your line-up and portfolio to utilise your fixed costs with a product with a low 'break-even' point. Therefore, 'downsized' publishing workforces have been made more 'flexible'. In this case this simply means being forced to take more work on, such as desk editors managing multiple journal titles under the *mantra* of working in a 'lean and mean' (but often simply 'anorexic') organisation.

Thus, we have publishers searching for ever-greater opportunities to publish. The launch of new journals, and the expansion of existing ones, are indicative of this.

Results: publication's paradoxes

These contextual conditions have produced a massive multiplication of articles submitted to editors, increased numbers of issues per journal volume and the launch of new journals. However, dissembling causation is tricky; like the 'chicken and the egg', as to which came first: (a) more articles = more journals, or (b) more journals = more articles. Nevertheless, there are both more forces to publish, and opportunities to get published. The results for editors are paradoxical. These include the following.

First, we have anecdotal evidence and stories of a litany of 'sharp' practices by some authors. These include the simultaneous submission of the same paper to different journals, the 'salami slicing' of research into several papers and very close 'versions' of papers being sent to different journals. Sometimes such practices come to light when these submissions are subsequently sent to the same referees by the different journals' editors! Another development is the growth of 'cheap and dirty' work that is premature in submission or based on, for example, MA or MBA projects. Another worrying 'method' is the deeply cynical approach of some authors who make the decision to submit deliberately incomplete papers to journals in the hope that referees will go to the trouble to suggest how to improve and even complete the paper for them!

Second, editors still have to deal delicately with academics whose egos and image of self-importance, is surprisingly matched by their 'thin skins'. This continues to amaze me. Any criticisms, let alone outright rejection, are often taken personally, and sometimes acrimoniously, and not at all with good grace. Such righteous indignation of authors can be difficult for editors to deal with and manage, especially where on-going professional (and sometimes even personal) relationships are involved, for example, if such authors are editorial board members, article referees, and so. There is also the problem for editors of trying to reconcile referees' conflicting reports or presenting their sometimes bitter and acerbic critiques in a more constructive and positive light for feedback to the authors.

Third, there is often less time (or interest) for many academics to be involved actually in the publication process chain. This ranges from editorship itself, to the 'unnamed soldiers' of the process – those referees who actually do a good job in increasingly difficult times. Trying to track down suitable and reliable referees is a more and more time-consuming (and often unrewarding) process for many editors. Many potential referees contacted simply do not give editors the courtesy of a reply, even if it is only to be a negative one. It is interesting that such non-responses often emanate from the very same insecure individuals characterised in the above two points.

Fourth, editors need to enhance their negotiation and political skills in dealing with publishers and desk editors in organisations increasingly run as hard-nosed businesses. Some publishers are trying (and too often sadly achieving) to displace increasing amounts and types of labour and work onto the academic editors themselves. Sometimes the tactic of trying to play-off joint editors against each other is used in this escapade. A united front is the best response, with solidarity between co-editors a prerequisite for dealing with publishers trying to 'whip-saw' them into taking on more work. Nevertheless, the 'frontier of responsibility' has become blurred, permeable and often then shifted. For instance, editors do not simply receive and rustle up papers, liaise with contributors, contact and cajole referees, seemingly pass judgement on the 'worth' of someone's work and deal with authors chasing up the non-appearance (or lateness) of their accepted articles. Further tasks increasingly pushed onto journal editors include ever closer and exact editing of papers into house-style, camera-ready copy, undertaking changes on disc and liaising with authors. These publication 'jobs' also stretch all the way through to marketing in various forms, from supplying publishers with lists to sending and taking fliers to conferences and acting ever more pro-actively!

All these trends in publishing are growing at a time when many departments are increasingly less likely to see any 'pay-off' in supporting an academic journal. After all, journal articles and research grants are the 'macho' measures of 'success' now. Thus, secretarial assistance and so on (if provided at all) for editors, is slimmed-down, de-emphasised or removed. This actually does not apply to my own institution. However, one interesting example of this process is of a department that now limits secretarial support for an academic journal using the bizarre measure of 5 per cent of a single (part-time) secretary's time. Even worse, this paltry figure has to be shared between three roles, with the academics concerned acting as two of the journal's editors and also the reviews editor. Can it really be useful, again using the previous case, to allocate just 1.66 per cent of a secretary's time per editor per week? This translates to just 8 minutes per day or 32 minutes per week per editor's job on the four-day week worked in this example. This situation obviously means the existing and extra tasks are forced onto journal editors who, let us not forget, as all too many contributors and publishers do, are very often actually full-time academics caught up in the same self-defeating spiral to 'publish or perish' as much of the rest of academia.

Conclusion

There are several main results from these developments and trends in publication for academic journal editorship. First, more and more is written, submitted and even published. Huge volumes of paper are shifted, dealt with and in transit at any one time. Yet, this is then often at the cost of 'never mind the quality feel the width' as less and less is actually read, let alone goes on to become referred to as a 'classic'. One common statistic banded about is that in the social sciences, articles are only read an average of 1.5 times! Second, many more academics want (or need) to publish more and demand quicker and quicker responses, decisions and turn-arounds from editors simply to fit in with arbitrary, and cyclically repeated assessment exercise deadlines. It would be interesting to track longitudinally the levels of submissions to see if there was any correlation with these cut-off dates.

Yet, at the same time as this time compression, with ever louder, veracious and persistent demands for swiftness on the journal editor's part, we have the paradox that many academics are less willing to become involved in the publication process, in terms of the actual refereeing of papers, or for many departments to assist in supporting editors. This is partly because this work is seen as not 'cost effective' in the increasingly self-centred and individualist career patterns being forged and exacerbated in contemporary academia. At times the whole editing system seems on the verge of crisis and becoming de-based with this academic fragmentation and division of labour.

Editors seem to fit the classic description of people 'stuck in the middle' of processes. For instance, in the work environment you often had 'charge-hands' and 'foremen' (*sic*), seen as the 'rubbing rags' between shopfloor workers and management. These people were often held in suspicion by both the employee and employer sides for being representatives of the 'other side', having 'gone native' and having become incorporated and assimilated. Many editors sit similarly perched between contributors and publishers in this classic pose. Yet, this is an increasingly uncomfortable and exposed position to remain in for any length of time. Having said all this, I should add that I am actually enjoying the position and am not yet ready for a one-way ticket out of the 'front line'.

Chapter 9

Writing for Refereed Journals and Conferences: the first few papers

by Martin Askey

Introduction

*T*HE aim of this chapter is to relate and analyse experiences of academic publishing and to demonstrate that gaining a reasonable publication record is not too difficult. The chapter is based on my first fours years as an academic during which time I have managed to publish four journal papers and four conference papers in between teaching and administrative duties. Before joining Napier University I contributed to a book, edited conference proceedings and completed a research MSc while working in industry.

Publication of Journal Papers – lessons learned

Choice of Journal

In every research field there is a hierarchy of journals and it is important that you recognise this. Your research experience should highlight the key journals for your subject and enable you to select appropriate targets for publication. Look for papers that are similar to something you might produce and take copies of them – the style, approach and content are all important. It is worth making contact with a journal to ask what sort papers they are looking for. Editors are normally willing to offer their views on this and often have particular likes and dislikes. You may find that the journal is planning to publish a series of papers in a similar area for one issue, and that this is the ideal opportunity to submit your work. If possible you should develop a relationship with an editor; simple enquiries may start a correspondence. Conferences are a valuable means of getting to know people; if an editor remembers you and has some background knowledge of your work he or she is more likely to accept your paper.

Remember that what one editor rejects another may welcome with open arms. Do not be disappointed if the editor dismisses your carefully crafted paper by writing, 'this material is not suitable for this journal'. This can sound very disheartening but it may be that the journal genuinely does not wish to focus in this area and the current editor wants to pursue other interests. A rejection of this nature does not necessarily reflect badly on the quality of your work, it may simply be poorly targeted. Wherever possible have your target journal in mind before starting to write rather than writing a paper and then searching for somewhere to publish it.

Try to identify who the referees are for a particular journal. It is unlikely that you will obtain names but it is usually possible to judge what type of people are involved. Imagine what qualities you would be looking for in a paper, think what they require, for example, format, type of material, house-style, level of analysis etc. By getting into the mind of the potential referees it is possible to referee your own paper before submission, thus improving its focus and likelihood of acceptance. A useful exercise is to review papers from colleagues or students.

Writing a Paper

Good subject matter will usually lead to a good paper provided that you follow some basic rules. When writing for a journal it is important to think about the audience for that particular publication and tailor your work for them. The same material can usually be presented in a number of different ways. For example, a research audience may value a highly theoretical approach with multiple references to previous work, full presentation of data, statistical techniques (if appropriate) and a particular style of writing that has developed over the years. A more practically oriented audience of people working in industry and commerce may be equally interested in your findings but may prefer them to be presented in a straight-forward pragmatic manner, for they are interested in what they will be able to do with the knowledge rather than how it relates to and advances the subject.

Good journal papers have focussed arguments and are supported by relevant facts. The author should think 'what is the point that I'm trying to make' and ensure that the work does not stray from this. It may be appropriate to separate some of the issues into a second paper if they tend to blur the main point of your argument.

When producing a paper you should think about the overall structure first and then fill in the detail. Writing the titles and sub-titles of the work allows you to see the overall structure clearly and so prevents you from straying from the point later on. Once the titles are in place, type in rough notes and the key facts to be brought out. You should allocate a word count to each section to ensure that you balance the work properly. This helps to give an overview of where the emphasis should be placed and shows whether any material ought to be added or deleted. These methods enable you to focus the work and concentrate on the message you want to deliver before you engage in the detailed writing.

With the use of a word-processor spelling and grammar should not be a problem. The overall format of the work will be determined by the requirements of the journal and it is important to comply with these. Remember that you are trying to convince the editor that your paper is worthy of publication and will reflect well on him or her; if you are unable to follow simple formatting instructions that editor's confidence may be dented and the paper rejected before it ever reaches the review stage.

Developing a good writing style is important and this will vary according to the type of publication and your field. This chapter is written in a very relaxed, personal style (relative to my normal work) because it is relating my personal experiences rather than actual research work. Journals have their own (often unstated) house-style and it is important to tune into this. The style is determined by the subject, historical factors, the readership, the editor and format amongst other things; try reading a few papers from a selection of journals and making a comparison. If the style of your paper does not match the journal the chances of rejection are much greater.

Working with a colleague for the first couple of papers is a great help. Joint authorship with someone more experienced has significant benefits for both parties. From the less experienced author's point of view you get help with style, editing and contacts with journals. The addition of a prestigious name to your paper may add credibility. From the experienced author's point of view there is always pressure to publish, so being able to get a journal publication on the basis of helping you to edit your work is a good deal – minimal effort for maximum gain. Remember that the first named author is normally taken as being the person who did the most work or who originated the paper and ensure that your citation reflects this fairly.

Submitting Your Paper

Although you might think that the quality of your paper should speak for itself, a good covering letter explaining the background and reasons why the paper should be published gives the editor a more positive impression. A brief letter could explain the key results and why you believe the work would be of interest to the readership. If you have already made contact with the editor to discuss your potential paper, gently remind him or her of this: remember, commitments or comments made over the telephone or at conferences by busy people are often forgotten. If you have developed a relationship with the editor it may be worth telephoning or sending an e-mail first to say that your submission is in the post.

Responses from Editors and Referees

Do not be disappointed if your paper is rejected by return of post. Your presubmission research should have avoided this but there can be many reasons why a paper is rejected and many of them are nothing to do with the quality of writing or research. Reply to the editor thanking him or her for their time and consideration and asking for a more detailed appraisal of why you were rejected so that you can take appropriate corrective action. Ask the editor who else may be interested in publication.

Getting to the stage of referees' comments is a good sign as many papers do not make it this far. Referees' comments will normally be returned with a covering letter from the editor explaining what action is required. It is unusual, at this stage, to get feedback indicating that the paper is entirely unsuitable (the editor would not normally allow such papers to be refereed) although some comments can be quite harsh.

Revising Papers (handling comments)

The most common situation is that the referees have made a number of comments that you are asked to respond to before publication can be reconsidered. Be positive about the referees' comments and try to see them as constructive. Remember that although each referee may be trying to show the editor how clever he or she is, the comments will still have some validity and must be answered. Editors are usually in the position that they cannot legitimately publish the paper unless the comments have been thoroughly addressed.

If there is more than one referee, compare what they say to get a general picture of their views. You may find conflicting opinions in the comments, which is always frustrating and demonstrates how subjective referees are. When revising the paper, systematically answer all the points, even if you disagree with them. Editors rely on the referees for their quality control and it is therefore unlikely that you will be able to convince them that the referees are wrong, particularly if their independent comments tally. If you feel, however, that there has been some misunderstanding do not change the paper un- necessarily. Remember that a referee is commenting not only as an expert but also as a first-time reader of the paper; if he or she has misinterpreted your paper it is likely that others will. Revise the paper so that the points are made in a strong, clear fashion. As there is often a delay in this process you may have some more up-to-date information to add to the paper at this stage. Work this material in and highlight to the editor that you have done this. This gives a positive impression of caring about the immediacy of the work and appears to be a bonus for the journal.

You should be able to respond to the comments fairly quickly – within a couple of weeks rather than a couple of months. When returning your revised paper thank the editor for the comments (even if you did not like them) and describe how the paper has been changed to cover them. Make it as easy as possible for the editor to see that you have addressed the points and improved the paper. If you do this, the editor can have some confidence in his or her quality control mechanism and be unlikely to send the paper back out for a second round of referee reports.

Conference Papers – lessons learned

National and international conferences do not rank highly in the Research Assessment Exercise (RAE). Attendance and presentation of papers at con- ferences does, however, provide a useful way of consolidating ideas, getting immediate peer feedback and meeting people in your specialised field.

A good way of both progressing and consolidating your current work is to formulate a draft paper that might be suitable for a conference. Writing in this style is a good research discipline because it focusses you on what you have achieved and what remains to be done. Ask the question 'what have I done that would be of interest to others?'. When a suitable call for papers appears your thoughts are already tuned to what you could contribute. You should never prepare a complete conference paper before the abstract has been selected as this allows you to tailor the content to the exact needs of the audience.

Choice of Conference

The choice of conference is important as there is a hierarchy within the conference circuit. Most conferences do not attract a high rating in the RAE so it makes more sense to use your own criteria for selection of appropriate events. Factors to consider include:

In What Type of Conference are You Interested?
In the management field there are two main types of conference – research presentations and training/consultancy. The former consists of reports of recent research work (usually in highly specialised areas) whereas the latter is more concerned in giving a practising audience an overview of particular topics. Presenting a pure research paper to an audience of practitioners looking for a pragmatic solution to their own problems is unlikely to be successful (and *vice versa*).

Where do Researchers You Admire Go?
When you review the literature in your area you will find that particular conferences turn up time after time. It makes sense to follow the lead of more experienced researchers until you have made more contacts. In some fields conferences consist of workshops and tutorials (some on an invitation-only basis) and these can be useful for making contacts.

Why do You Want to Go?
Your reason for wishing to present a paper at the conference may affect your choice of event. Reasons for attending conferences can include the making of new contacts, generation of business or research contacts, accumulation of papers for RAE, free trip to somewhere exotic and so on.

Practicality – money
Presenting papers at conferences is normally an expensive business particularly when compared to the minimal costs involved in journal publication. Costs include travel, accommodation, subsistence and conference fees. If you have a fixed budget it is important that you assess the value-for-money that you receive from the conference. You may find that money spent on a conference could be better employed in advancing your research and publishing a journal paper. If you have to obtain money from various sources (grants, departmental funds etc.), good justification and cost benefit analysis is required.

Is it an Attractive Venue?

It seems perfectly reasonable to select your conference using the venue as one of the differentiating criteria. Many conference organisers recognise the fact that delegates wish to see the surrounding area during their visit and make provision for this with free time in the programme and/or organised visits. Flights to European destinations are often cheaper if a weekend is included giving you the ideal excuse for extending the conference into a holiday.

Developing an Abstract

Conferences place calls for papers up to eighteen months in advance of the event. An abstract of your proposed paper is usually requested and this short document will determine whether you are accepted for the conference or not. It is, therefore, important that this document is prepared carefully; your paper is commissioned on the basis of the abstract. Some factors to consider are as follows:

Read the Call for Papers Carefully

What are the main topics being highlighted? Target your abstract to a particular subject that is central to the conference theme. In this way you give the conference organisers positive reasons to include your work – a good paper that does not fit in with the overall theme is unlikely to be accepted. Ensure that you comply with the administrative requirements, such as the number of words required, conference language(s), number of copies required, final submission date and additional information required.

Get Inside the Conference Organiser's Mind

Many conferences appear to be huge events with a long list of prestigious advisers; in fact they are often run by a small group of individuals who are overworked and quite anxious to have a successful event. Think what they want to see in the paper and what would make them feel confident that your paper or presentation will reflect well on them; the organisers are trying to minimise the risk of accepting a disastrous speaker. Key factors include: a good title, key words matching those in the call for papers, evidence of past performance and support from established figures in the field (it may be worth trying a joint paper with someone more experienced or senior to start with).

Remember that the abstract at this stage is a sales pitch and that once your abstract has been accepted it is unlikely that your completed paper will be rejected. Making contact with the organiser before submitting an abstract ensures a better reception and enables you to gauge more precisely what is required. In addition, a good covering letter highlighting the key features of your work, its relevance to the audience and your experience is worth taking some care over. You are trying to convince the organisers that you have a good paper that will not let them down.

Responses from the Conference Organisers

Your abstract will be reviewed by referees and this process can vary enormously. There is a move towards full, independent refereeing of papers in most academic conferences but industry or trade conferences may simply rely on the head of the organising committee reading your abstract and discussing it with one of his or her colleagues. Conferences with a systematic refereeing approach will usually obtain reports from two referees on each paper and use a standard form to report this. The confidentiality of authors and referees is normally preserved throughout this process.

Bear in mind who the referees might be and how they are likely to view your submission. As with journal papers, the referees may be trying to demonstrate their superiority to the conference organiser.

If your abstract is rejected ask for a reason, if this has not already been provided. It may be that your paper was good but that there were too many other abstracts submitted (in which case you should look for another conference) or you may have missed the target with regard to what the organisers required. In the latter case it is important that you understand the reasons behind this to avoid the same mistake in the future.

If your abstract is accepted do not give up the right to develop material over a longer period; presentation at a conference can be seen as a stepping stone towards developing a more advanced journal paper. Ensure that you understand the administrative arrangements with regard to submission of the full paper and registration for the conference.

Take the opportunity to be involved in organising a conference if this presents itself, even a minor event (national or regional). Being part of the organising side gives you an insight into selection criteria adopted, reasons for accepting or rejecting work, the pressures facing a conference committee, the problems that disorganised speakers cause and the main factors affecting speaker performance. While working in industry I became involved in the organisation of an industry sector conference, giving me a valuable insight into the way conference organisers work and also provided an opportunity to be the editor of the conference proceedings. Acting as editor gave me first hand experience of receiving late, poorly focussed and badly edited material.

Constructing the Paper

With your abstract accepted you can now start work on the detailed text and presentation. The scale of this task will vary depending on how far advanced your work was beforehand. The most important part of a conference is the audience and ensuring that the message they receive is clear and reflects well on your abilities. Many good pieces of research are spoilt by poor presentation whereas a good presentation of poor or simplified research can receive a rapturous reception.

If the conference organisers intend to publish proceedings, remember that the written paper is different from a good presentation. Your written paper can be quite brief and should provide the reader with the details of the whole piece of work whereas the presentation may focus on particular aspects in detail. Bear in mind that the paper may be read by people who have not attended the conference.

Attending the Conference

Presentation
Before making the presentation always check the venue – room size, acoustics, provision of audio-visual equipment etc. Make a point of meeting the chairman/woman and other speakers well before the session. If you have the option of using a microphone then take it; there is nothing worse for an audience than not being able to hear the speaker. Lapel microphones work well but make sure that it is not brushing against anything as you move and that it is close enough to your mouth to be effective.

Handling Questions
There is usually an opportunity for the audience to ask questions at the end of each paper or in a plenary session. Always answer the person directly and to their face. Be brief but precise. Its embarrassing not to get any questions so brief the session chairman/woman with one or two suitable, general questions that he or she can use if necessary.

Making Contacts
One of the many benefits of attending conferences is the opportunity to make

contacts with a wide range of people. There are several ways in which this can happen.

If, as speaker, you manage to engage the audience's interest, people are likely to come up to you after the presentation and ask for copies of your overheads or express an interest in collaboration. Therefore go prepared by taking business cards to hand out and remember to collect cards from interested people. On the cards you have collected make notes of what the person wants and then follow them up immediately you return to base.

When you are listening to other papers you may come across work that is of great interest to you. Try to talk to the speaker after the presentation but remember that this may be rushed and the speaker may not be able to give you their full attention. Write on your card what you want (copies of OHPs, opportunity to talk, etc.) and give it to them. If the opportunity arises later in the conference catch the speaker at a quiet moment; most people are more than willing to spend some time discussing their work with a genuinely interested person.

Planning for Future Publications

Plan and manage your research with publication in mind. A schedule of research work should include a publication plan that identifies potential journals and conferences by name. Career advancement in academia is driven by publication at this time; although senior staff state that promotion is based on balanced performance in the areas of teaching, research and administration it is clear that those with a good research publication record do very well.

Sources of material are many and varied and do not have to be based on funded research programmes. Good papers can be been based on (very) part-time research with no funding. Personal PhD or post-doctoral research is always a good source of material and you should expect to get at least one conference and one journal paper per year from this source. My MSc thesis was used as the source for two papers, both of which were published in international refereed journals, and these were prepared in co-operation with my MSc supervisor, Dr Barrie Dale. His wealth of experience enabled me to publish in reputable journals very early in my academic career and provided a firm platform on which to build. In addition to this he was preparing a text book on quality management and invited me to develop some of my MSc material into a chapter. Although this type of writing does not rank highly in research assessment terms it is very pleasant to see yourself in a proper textbook for the first time.

Lower level research work is also useful, particularly where several projects are complementary. For example, student projects (post- and undergraduate) can result in publication if the work is carried out well and the aims and objectives are considered carefully. Recently a particularly good undergraduate project lead to a successful journal publication and this approach had benefits for both the student and me, with the former using this work as part of a successful grant application to study in the United States. Another student project (this time at MSc level) provided the basis for a conference paper. The thesis submitted by the student was not particularly well focussed but the subject matter matched a call for papers for a national conference. This presented an ideal opportunity to develop another publication but, more importantly, to give the student the opportunity to consolidate the work into a presentation. I edited the thesis into a draft paper and added some extra material; the student carried out further development work and prepared a presentation. In addition to pure academic work, consultancy projects for commercial organisations are the perfect source of up-to-date case study material.

Remember that subject fashions will change and that the target audience's taste will be determined by this. Keep abreast of trends and try to focus on the current issues that people are interested in. Valuable research in deeply unfashionable subjects may never be published whereas less rigorous work at the forefront of public attention may succeed.

The Research Assessment Exercise criteria that universities are now subject to has a strong influence on publication. At least 50 per cent of the assessment is based on publication performance, and maximum credit is gained for refereed international journal papers. This mechanism for measuring research performance has attracted a lot of criticism and comment but looks likely to remain in place in the immediate future. Some academics are actively striving to achieve the minimum number of journal papers required at any cost and the amount of competition to get published is increasing. A balanced approach to conferences, journals and books seems to be becoming lost in the rush to obtain a higher rating in this system; from the individual researcher's point of view this could be a bad thing. For the young researcher, conferences have many benefits including making contacts in the research community and this is in danger of being lost. Likewise, the publication of a book is a longer-term, high input task which only receives similar credit to one short journal paper (in the RAE approach). Publishing a book does, however, have considerable value because of its more rounded approach. To summarise, building your research (publication) CV should be a balanced affair taking advantage of all the approaches available.

Lessons Learned So Far

To summarise my experience so far I have compiled a list of 'what to do' and 'what not to do'.

Journal Papers

- Do not ignore the format rules for the journal.
- Do select target journals carefully.
- Do not forget who your audience is.
- Do make contact with the editors wherever possible.
- Do not give up if rejected from your first journal.

Conference Papers

- Do take the opportunity to get involved in organising a conference.
- Do not submit abstracts to conferences that you cannot attend.
- Do take the time to produce a good abstract.
- Do not forget to check the venue – size, AV facilities etc.
- Do read the conference instructions.
- Do not simply read the text of your paper.
- Do speak to the conference organisers directly.
- Do not try to do too much in the presentation time available.
- Do take plenty of business cards.
- Do not run over time – audiences get remarkably impatient, even over one or two minutes extra.

Publication in General

- Do react positively to referees' comments.
- Do not be disappointed if you are rejected – it does not mean that someone else will not welcome your contribution enthusiastically.
- Do develop a publication plan (about 2 years in advance).
- Do not get too engrossed with the RAE criteria – take a more rounded approach.
- Do pick the journal or conference before starting to write.

Chapter 10

Other Publication Outlets:
is there life after refereed journals?

by Mark Griffiths

*T*HIS chapter aims to look at writing for non-refereed outlets and show how publishing in such outlets can be of benefit to the academic. I make no apology for the fact that many of the examples in the chapter come from my own personal experience as these are the experiences which have put me in a position to write such a chapter as this! However, before starting, I would like to make the following assertions which I feel are important to the debate surrounding publishing in non-refereed outlets.

- Most academics would agree that the findings of their research should be disseminated as widely as possible.
- Academics who disseminate their work in non-refereed outlets (non-academic books, magazine and newspaper articles) may be ridiculed by their peers and/or told that such activities are of little use for progression in their academic career.

I would be the first to admit that these assertions have been made without any empirical evidence, but if they are true – and I believe passionately that they are – they may in part help to explain why most academics are reluctant to publish outside of the refereed journal arena. There is of course, more recently, the additional pressure to publish in refereed journals being placed on academics by the Research Assessment Exercise (RAE). However, even before the RAE's increasing impact, the assertions I outlined at the beginning probably held some validity. I should also add that I am not trying to play down the fundamental importance of peer review and/or refereed journal publications. Such publications are crucial in the career of any academic, but what I want to argue in this chapter is that publishing in non-refereed outlets can be done *alongside* refereed academic publishing.

Instead of viewing an article in a newsletter or a magazine as a 'second rate' outlet, we as academics should surely be trying to make our work as accessible as possible to the widest and largest number of audiences. Some academic subjects are of course 'sexier' than others in that they have wide audience appeal. In that respect I am probably one of the fortunate ones in that my areas of academic research include behavioural addictions (for example, sex addiction, Internet addiction), gambling (for example, National Lottery, scratchcards, fruit machines), interactive technology (computer games, Internet, virtual reality), and the psychology of fame. To some extent I have 'chosen' these areas but some seem to have fallen fortuitously into my lap. Whatever the reason, the most important thing is that I have capitalized on these areas in terms of academic writing and disseminated my research findings to as many people as possible in a diverse set of writings. Occasionally this will backfire when I write something for (say) a magazine and a sub-editor gives my article a 'sensationalized' headline that overplays the research findings (for example, "Joystick junkies"). However, if the headline persuades people to read my article, then the headline has (to some extent) served its function and the information about my research is successfully disseminated to a much wider readership than a refereed journal.

The 'Research Assessment Exercise' Culture

There is no doubt that the increasing importance of the Research Assessment Exercise makes it less likely that an academic would want to publish in non-refereed outlets. However, I personally do not think that our academic lives should be totally governed by the RAE culture. The RAE raises important questions of what our function as academic researchers should be.

In my own discipline, some academics (for example, Kremer, 1997) have made a plea for the discipline to pause a while and consider the damage which the exercise is inflicting on United Kingdom psychology. Many see the RAE as a game to play and as Kremer (345) points out, 'If we continue to subscribe to the maxim that "this is the only game in town" *then it will be the only game in town* (my emphasis) and, winners and losers alike, the psychological community will suffer the consequences'. This is not a healthy state of affairs and I would argue that one of our most important functions is to carry out scholarly activity which we then communicate and disseminate to as wide an audience as possible. Some people may disagree with the final part of the last statement as I can certainly think of academics who only want their work to be appreciated by the favoured few (usually other people in their research area).

Types of Outlet

There are many different outlets that an academic can publish in and many different types of academic writing. This chapter does not concern itself with textbook writing, writing book chapters, technical and/or internal reports, book reviews and abstracts as these are deemed to be legitimate scholarly outlets, even if the RAE perceives them to be of less benefit than papers in refereed journals. Although the list below is not exhaustive it contains what I feel to be the main sources of other forms of academic dissemination:

- Papers for professional and vocational journals
- Articles and brief reports for bulletins and newsletters
- 'Faction' writing for novels
- Articles for newspapers and magazines
- Letters to national newspapers

Apart from wider dissemination, there are many other benefits to writing non-refereed papers which I shall discuss during the rest of this chapter. Before going on to discuss these in more detail I should say there are further indirect benefits of writing for non-refereed outlets. The main ones (at least in my own personal experience) include a wide range of opportunities to do other things. Most (if not all) include invitations such as:

- giving keynote papers at academic conferences, workshops and/or learned societies
- giving seminar papers at other institutions (universities, colleges etc.) or outside agencies (for example, health authorities, education authorities, local councils)
- reviewing books for magazines and journals
- writing book chapters
- appearing on radio and television programmes (local, national and/ or international)
- opportunities for consultancies

I cannot claim that such invitations are purely as a result of writing for non-refereed outlets but they are certainly contributory. All of these activities are to some extent self-perpetuating and very inter-linked. To give you a very explicit example I would like to tell you about one experience of mine which is in no way unique.

Case Example 1

Back in April 1995 I was giving a paper on 'technological addictions' (about my research on addictions to computer games and slot machines) at the British Psychological Society Annual Conference. A month before the conference I came across an article in *The New York Times* about people supposedly 'hooked' on the Internet. This kind of 'addiction' was one which fitted my theoretical ideas about technological addictions. As a consequence, I joined an addiction discussion group and there asked for any comments on the phenomenon of 'Internet addiction' from other Internet users. Within days I had received five or six replies from people who considered themselves to be 'addicted' to the Internet.

At the conference, I produced a few of the anecdotal excerpts from the 'net addicts' during my paper. The press then got hold of the story (or created one!) and all they wanted to know about was 'Internet addiction' rather than my empirical work on other addictions. As a result of all the press coverage, I was asked to write a 1,800-word article for *The Times Higher Education Supplement* and since its publication in April 1995 I have never looked back. Internet addiction is now one of my main research areas and I have written on this area both academically in refereed journals and in other outlets such as professional journals (*Clinical Psychology Forum*), newspapers (for example, *The Sun*) and magazines (for example, *The Web, net*).

Obviously much that I have written so far in this section comes down to publicity on some level and I would argue that this can help in every area, from student recruitment at your university to your own self standing and reputation. I will return to the theme of publicity later in this chapter.

Choosing the Publication Outlet

If you decide that there is more to your academic research career than just writing papers for refereed journals then you need to decide which outlet you are going to choose and have some justification for your chosen option. If you really do not know what is out there then the best (and most profitable) thing you can do is to go and spend some time browsing in the library (for professional/vocational journals, newsletters) and/or a large newsagent (for newspapers and magazines) to get a clear idea of the available writing markets. Another additional but very worthwhile option is to read the *Writers and Artists Yearbook* which provides comprehensive lists of newspapers and magazines in the United Kingdom.

When you have decided on the outlet you would like to try writing for, it is a good idea to read the chosen publication very carefully in order to get a feel of the 'house-style' and to give you a rough guide to any word limits. If you really look around you will be surprised how many outlets might be able to feature your work.

Writing Papers for Professional and Vocational Journals

Professional and vocational journals do not appear to be given much weight when it comes to the RAE but they are an ideal way of getting across applications of your research to a much wider audience. One of the main advantages of writing about applications of your research in professional journals is that you can often get more than one publication out of the same piece of research. This does not mean *publishing the same piece of work twice* but means writing other articles based on research findings. The number of spin-offs from one piece of research obviously depends on the subject matter. In my own discipline of psychology, an academic could carry out a piece of research and maximise the number of outputs by writing papers which highlight specific psychological aspects of the research findings (for example, social psychology, developmental psychology, cognitive psychology, psycho-biology etc.). On a more specific level, one of my research areas is the area of adolescent gambling addiction. The great thing about this area is that you can do a piece of research and then ask yourself what the implications of your findings are to many different professional and vocational areas (for example, law, probation, social work, social policy) all of which have their own discipline-specific journals. I am also lucky that this area is media-friendly and can be written up journalistically. It could be the case that I am very lucky in both terms of my discipline and specific research areas, but I would imagine that most academics could maximise their writing outputs if they thought carefully about disseminating to more than one audience.

Writing Articles and Brief Reports for Bulletins and Newsletters

Publication outlets such as bulletins and newsletters are an ideal way of publishing work in progress, speculative thoughts or just communicating to people in your academic field that you are interested in a particular academic area. An advantage of publishing in these types of outlet is that the hit rate of getting something accepted is a lot higher, which means the rewards are more reinforcing than many of the rejections that academics get from the top refereed journals. This can be particularly useful for both postgraduates and junior lecturers starting out in their academic career.

Another advantage of these types of outlets is that the academic can often produce a variety of different kinds of writing. For instance, the British Psychological Society produces its own magazine, (*The Psychologist*) monthly, in addition to numerous publication outlets for both its many divisions and sections (for example, *Clinical Psychology Forum, Social Psychological Review, Education Section Review, The Occupational Psychologist, The Developmental Psychology Section Newsletter*). *The Psychologist* has many different sections all of which I regularly try to write things for. These include writing articles for the 'Research in Brief' section (in which authors provide short summaries of recently published research), the 'Students' page (in which authors provide articles of use to postgraduate students), the 'Lighter Side' (in which authors provide humorous pieces of writing) and the 'News' section (in which authors can write about anything of general interest such as reports of conferences they have attended). As you can see, those of us in psychology have many outlets to write for. In other disciplines there may not be as many types of outlet but most disciplines who have some kind of professional society will have their own magazine, bulletin and/or newsletter.

'Faction' Writing in Novels

Many people may claim they cannot get their ideas across unless it is done in a popularising format. The question of how to popularise ideas has led noted academics to incorporate such knowledge into works of fiction. I learned quite a lot about literary criticism from reading the literary works of David Lodge. Further to this, it inspired me to go and read more of Lodge's academic-based work in addition to other writers' work such as Terry Eagleton. The same kind of trend can be observed in the relationship between philosophy and literature where it could perhaps be claimed that the novel has always been better than a textbook for popularising philosophical ideas. Much has been made of the best selling *Sophie's World* by Jostein Gaarder. The plot revolves around a teenage girl, Sophie, who starts receiving mysterious letters which ask big questions ('Who are you?', 'Where does the world come from?' etc.) and goes on to answer them by summarizing the history of Western philosophy. The book is not new to the genre in that it has a number of antecedents (for example, Goëthe, Dostoyevsky, Proust, Sartre, Umberto Eco etc.) but it is unusual for such a book to be at the top of the best-seller lists. (However, I do realise that topping the best-seller lists does not necessarily imply that everyone has read it. For instance, how many people can honestly say they got past the first couple of chapters in Stephen Hawking's *The Brief History of Time*?) What I am trying to argue is that popularization is easier in spheres that people are used to and have ready access to, and that academics should not ignore this type of outlet if what they are interested in is getting across difficult ideas and concepts.

Writing Letters to National Newspapers

Writing letters to national newspapers may seem a little out of place in an academic context but I would like to argue that it can be very beneficial and can stimulate research into cutting-edge topics. According to Kline (1988), the content of newspapers provides a useful indicant of human behaviour. Newspapers indicate what people actually do, and they indicate what editors believe people like to read about. Most (and some would say all) of my current research areas have been influenced by the media to some extent (for example, the National Lottery and scratchcard gambling, Internet addiction, virtual reality, technology and crime, fame etc.). I would like to share with you a very clear example of how writing a letter to a national newspaper stimulated my interest to carry out research into a new area – namely that of scratchcard gambling.

Case Example 2

Since 1988 I have published numerous papers on 'fruit machine addiction' but I would be the first to admit that I do not know very much about scratchcards. In March 1995, *Camelot* introduced their instant scratchcards and I was asked to comment on them by various members of the media. I remember describing them to journalists as 'paper fruit machines' which seemed to catch on. However, just because a newspaper prints your comments, it does not automatically make you an expert in a particular subject. However, the journalists stimulated my thinking about the psychological nature of scratchcards and as a consequence, my views started to become polarized to the extent that I penned a letter to *The Times*. In April 1995 I was lucky enough to get an edited version of my letter published. Later that afternoon I got a call from a London radio station asking if I would appear on their breakfast show the next morning to talk about the letter I had published. The next day I did a live interview on the breakfast show and as a result of this interview, parts of which were repeated on the half hour news bulletins, I was suddenly inundated with requests for interviews with other radio stations. This was the 'snowball effect' in action. Within about a month I had done about fifteen interviews on scratchcards and somehow established myself as the 'expert' in the area. The only problem was I had never written anything academically about scratchcards except for the letter! As a consequence, I researched the area more fully and wrote an article on scratchcards and sent it off to a journal. Thankfully the journal accepted it almost immediately. The article was then quoted (almost *verbatim*) by the Labour MP Lynne Jones and appeared in *Hansard* – the proceedings of Parliament. I then put a successful grant bid together and am now engaged in a three-year study of adolescent scratchcard (and National Lottery) gambling. This is not my only example, as similar experiences have happened to me when I have written to newspapers about such subjects as Internet gambling, keno and Tamagotchis (cyberpets).

Before going on to examine writing articles for newspapers and magazines I am going to outline a brief history of the relationship between academia and the media.

The Relationship between Academia and the Media

Historically, the relationship between academia and the media has never been an easy one to bridge. Take, for example, the well known television anthropologist Desmond Morris. Morris was once a respected academic and like all his contemporaries was developing an academic research career (which in Morris' case was studying the 10-spined stickleback). Morris' move into television came about because of his desire to study apes. He gave up his research into sticklebacks to co-ordinate the running of a zoo film unit. This eventually brought him a television audience and he decided that when given the chance to disseminate knowledge, he would rather 'get one fact across to four million people than a hundred facts across to four people'. Such a polarized view lies at the heart of the 'dissemination' debate, that is, who should disseminate such knowledge and how should it be done?

Further to this, Morris has claimed in the national press that the problem of popularising is very difficult because such writing primarily involves simplification without distortion. Not only does he claim that popular writing is very hard to do but he asserts that it is much easier to be an academic because they can go into every minute detail. When Morris crossed over into the study of human behaviour, it was perhaps unsurprising that he became unpopular among other anthropologists and psychologists. The fact that he has made a lot of money out of such popularizations did nothing to increase his credibility and status. Nigel Barley (author of the *Innocent Anthropologist*) attacked Morris further by claiming he is 'popularising ideas that have been around for years. He's packaged them well, but really it's pretty low grade stuff. I hope he's laughing all the way to the bank, because if he takes it seriously I feel a bit sorry for him'.

I would argue that Morris' story is not untypical of those who decide to go down the popularising route. It is quite evident that there is still a lot of snobbery from academics about the rise of the media don. Even those people who continue to be academics but popularise their work come in for much criticism (Roger Penrose, Richard Dawkins, Colin Blakemore and Simon Schama, to name but a few). For instance, one unnamed academic quoted in an *Observer* article said 'These people discredit the profession. Academic discourse is considered, qualified, recognises shades of grey. The media see everything in black and white. How can you do justice to a complex subject in a 90-second soundbite?' (Gilligan, 1994). David Starkey, another of the leading media dons, responds that the only way to get some ideas across is to 'wrap them in tinsel'. The question we need to ask ourselves concerns how such a state of affairs arises and what our role as academics is in relation to the dissemination of our findings. Thankfully, White *et al.* (1993) argue that the climate of opinion in the British scientific community is slowly changing and that the public understanding of science is becoming a valued aim.

Writing Articles for Newspapers and Magazines

Traditionally scientists were not interested in explaining their work to a wider public (White *et al.*, 1993). There has always been a view (which to some extent almost certainly still exists) that attempting to popularise one's work *via* the media was not a 'proper' academic activity. However, writing for magazines or newspapers might provoke far less horror than it used to although White *et al.* assert there is still some envy among academics.

Some of the advantages of these types of outlets include being able to disseminate information far more widely than in academic journals and the more obvious bonus of getting paid for a written contribution.

If you want to write for a magazine or newspaper, then the best thing to do is send the editor a brief proposal outlining your idea(s) and 'make your pitch'. Editors normally know instantly whether an idea is worth pursuing, so do not waste time writing an article unless you are certain it will get published. Although newspapers and magazines occasionally accept unsolicited articles, they are the exception rather than the rule. If your idea for an article (or the article itself) is turned down it may be nothing to do with the quality of it. It may simply be that it does not fit in with the feel of the publication. Although there are a lot of similarities in writing for newspapers and magazines, there are some very distinct differences. The next section concentrates on writing for these two types of publication.

Writing Articles for Magazines

It is probably true to say that magazines (perhaps with the odd exception) are often not considered by academics as vehicles to publicise their work. The great thing about magazines is that there are so many of them and editors have pages to fill. This gives academics a lot of major outlets to publish their work in a communicable form. With sizeable and/or specially-interested readerships they can offer a highly effective channel into the public arena. If you are going to write an article for a magazine there are a few golden rules (see White *et al.*, 1993, for a more comprehensive overview):

- Start with a 'hook' (for example, a vivid case study or unusual event) to grip your readers.
- Use quotes and anecdotes to relieve the look of the copy.
- Use contemporary events to hang features on.
- Avoid jargon (except where absolutely necessary).
- Keep sentences short and match the appropriate house-style of the magazine.
- Be explicit about the nature of the article (What is the story? What are the central points?).
- Keep within the word length as sub-editors will hack down the article to fit within their space demands.

White *et al.* also claim it helps if your article

(1)   is original;
(2)   is being said for the first time;
(3)   affects thousands of people;
(4)   is worrying;
(5)   is controversial, different or amusing.

Writing Articles for Newspapers

Since academics are often asked to write features for newspapers about topical events, we must learn to write quickly. Although such feature articles allow the writer to be a little bit more technical than the average news report, the article still has to readable for a lay audience. In these types of articles newspaper editors often have a preference for the academic to have polarized views because this is likely to initiate debate.

Getting into the national newspapers is only achieved by a very small number of academics so one option which White *et al.* recommend is that of exploiting your geographical location. Basically, local newspapers love local news stories so I personally would aim to get something into my daily local evening paper (i.e. *Nottingham Evening Post*).

The Benefits of Writing Journalistically

Over the years, I have written a number of articles all of which have to varying degrees argued that most academics do not like the way that academic issues are portrayed in the media (for example, Griffiths, 1995a; 1995b). I have also tried to argue that most academics do not want any kind of relationship with the media because of the perception that they somehow trivialize and/or misrepresent serious research. The main problem that is perceived is that many people, both those reporting and those reading the original research, fail to interpret research findings of academics accurately, or use the findings in a biased and/or selective manner. Such an observation may provide a reason why an increasing number of academics are popularizing their own work themselves, that is, they do not want their work misunderstood, distorted and trivialized. However, if such a practice is not valued by the majority of academic peers, there is little incentive for the academic to do so.

Writing for the media can play a beneficial role in research and academia, and that a lot of good things can come out of it. Why can writing for the media perform a useful service for academics? I consider that

(1)   writing journalistically can provide publicity for the academic, the research, the discipline and the academic's institution;
(2)   writing journalistically can provide immediate rewards;
(3)   writing journalistically can feed back into the academic process.

I will now expand on these assertions a little further.

Writing Journalistically can Provide Publicity

Many academics may take the line that it is not their job to generate publicity for themselves or their institution. However, all universities have some kind of press and public relations office and I personally think that publicity can help an individual and/or their institution in a number of ways.

Participants for Research Studies

As I have always been told by one of my colleagues, 'it pays to advertise'. Although there are ethical questions to consider, news items and features in all forms of the media can help in either the recruitment of participants both in general calls for help in research and in terms of unsolicited responses. For instance, I have found this particularly useful in obtaining case studies for various behavioural addictions that I have been researching into (for example, exercise addiction, gambling addiction, Internet addiction etc.).

Reputation and Self-standing

I would also argue that being a media commentator in a particular research specialism raises one's own self-standing in that particular research area. I would also add that from my own personal experience that invitations from other places (for example, seminar speaker invitations) appear to increase and I have had more articles published than I would have done by not having a high media profile.

Immediate Rewards

One thing that really irritates me about the whole academic process is how slow it is. Sometimes waiting over a year or two for a paper to be published is not my idea of a quick reward! At least with journalistic writing the reinforcers can come very quickly. If you publish something in a newspaper or a magazine, it can be out within days and sometimes even hours. I would also argue that it is nice to be asked to do these kind of things and to be perceived as an 'expert' in our areas. Many may consider the education and dissemination of academic knowledge an important part of the academic occupation yet popularizing academic research appears to have no distinct advantages inside the academic system particularly when most universities are dominated by playing the Research Assessment Exercise game.

In my own discipline of psychology there are many psychologists who are very good at popularizing their own work and can communicate with both the general public and their peers (Griffiths, 1995a). Historically, people like Freud, Watson and Skinner spring to mind. In fact, Skinner and Watson both wrote articles for women's magazines (Murphy, John and Brown, 1984). However, an academic psychologist writing an article in the latest edition of magazines such as *Bella* or *Woman's Weekly* would probably be deeply frowned upon or ridiculed if repeated in today's academic climate. I personally hope that one day, academia may actually reward individuals for media contributions.

Feedback into the Academic Process

Overall, the main things which I feel I gain from writing journalistic articles are:

(1) a changed perception of how the media works and operates which has allowed me to be more tolerant when dealing with the media;
(2) an enhancement of my self-presentation skills (for example, telephone interviewing, patience);
(3) a way of working that is 'fast and furious', and where every second counts leading to increased productivity (particularly in terms of writing);
(4) improved information facilitation and comprehension;
(5) improved communication skills with people; and
(6) an increased capacity for genuine collaborative teamwork.

A Final Comment

I hope I have demonstrated that writing for non-refereed publication outlets can have positive outcomes on the whole. I would be the first to admit that things can go wrong occasionally but these are far outweighed by all the positive advantages. I realise that my own case examples will not be applicable to all but I hope I have given everyone reading this some insight into the possible benefits of writing outside the peer review process.

References

Gilligan, A. (1994) "Brains and corn", *The Observer*, October 7th.

Griffiths, M.D. (1995a) "'Pop' psychology", *The Psychologist: Bulletin of the British Psychological Society*, 8: 455-7.

Griffiths, M.D. (1995b) "A life in 'aca-media'", *Psy-PAG Quarterly*, 17:13-7.

Griffiths, M.D. (1997) "Media mayhem", *Psy-PAG Quarterly*, 23:10-3.

Kline, P. (1988) *Psychology Observed or The Emperor's New Clothes.* London: Routledge.

Kremer, J. (1997) "RAE: Enough is enough", *The Psychologist: Bulletin of the British Psychological Society*, 10: 344-5.

Murphy, J., John, M. and Brown, H. (1984) *Dialogues and Debates in Social Psychology*. Sussex: Erlbaum.

White, S., Evans, P., Mihill, C. and Tysoe, M. (1993) *Hitting the Headlines: A Practical Guide to the Media*. Leicester: British Psychological Society.

Chapter 11

The Final Word?

by Philip Hills

THIS book has been about the process of writing papers for refereed journals and other publication outlets. Since the first edition of this book some ten years ago a number of significant changes have taken place, in particular the pressure of the next Research Assessment Exercise. The success of departments in getting funding is dependant on the grading they receive and this in turn is very dependant on the excellence of staff research and their publications.

Largely as a result of the increased flow of papers occasioned by the Research Assessment Exercise, the number of paper-based journals has increased, their excellence (or otherwise) being measured by their 'impact factor' which is determined by the number of papers in them that are cited by others.

Possible electronic outlets for academic papers is also increasing dramatically. Existing paper-based journals now often have electronic versions available and there are many fully refereed journals that exist in electronic form only.

The use of e-mail and electronic discussion groups should also be noted here as they allow a rapid interchange of ideas and feedback on draft versions of a paper, the electronic equivalent of the old 'scientist's letters'.

One could argue that the actual process of writing papers has changed little. This however is not entirely true since the use of computers actually changes the *way* we write. Chapters 3 and 4 both consider aspects of this. Some people still prefer to produce a handwritten version of their paper first as their writing and their thought processes are better matched than perhaps their thoughts and their keyboard skills.

In practice there are now other ways of inputting one's thoughts to a computer, that is by voice and handwriting recognition. The voice recognition programme I have on my own computer will give a reasonable result if words are spoken separately and distinctly. Later programs now claim to capture continuous speech.

This part of the present chapter was written on my hand-held computer by using a handwriting program that I have just acquired. Again it seems to respond best to the inputting of one or two words at a time, but as we know all of these things are being improved or changed with frightening rapidity. There are distinct differences in the process of writing when using the keyboard, voice recognition or handwriting. For my own part I still prefer to scribble my first version on a piece of paper, using the input to a computer as a re-drafting tool.

In producing this second edition of *Publish or Perish* we have tried to include the basic information that you will need both to write a successful paper and to get it published. Chapters 1 and 9 will help you to get into the mind of the editor while Chapter 8 highlights the problems and doubts that the beginning author can go through. Chapter 10 extends our possible range of publications by reminding us that there are more publishing outlets out there than just refereed journals.

What of the Future?

In the short term little will change. Computers will run faster programs, voice recognition and handwriting programs will get better. It will be up to each one of us to find the methods of generating text that are most comfortable for us. Paper-based journals will continue to be published and electronic journals will continue to increase in number.

In the longer term the electronic version of the book in a convenient hand-held version will so develop to the extent that it may in some ways replace the original paper-based product, offering the electronic advantages of hyper-text links to other material, word and literature searches etc. However, snuggling up to a hand-held computer does not have quite the same appeal as a good read with a paper-backed book. Paper also, if carefully looked after, is reasonably indestructible but electronic files may not be, and as I write, a friend has just sent me a warning about yet another virus that can wipe all the data from your hard-drive!

Whatever happens, the academic will still be disseminating the results of his or her research via journals, books and reports albeit electronic or paper-based. One great advantage that electronic transmission offers is the speed of transfer so that we can quickly reach our particular community of scholars around the world, getting comments and ideas from them much more rapidly than in the past. Perhaps sometime in the near future we shall be able to elaborate more fully on this aspect in a third edition of *Publish or Perish*.

And Finally!

As an absolutely final word the following is a copy of an article recently published in the *British Medical Journal* (BMJ vol. 317, 26th September 1998) and reproduced here with kind permission. It illustrates two of the main aspects of publishing your research:

(1)   It is possible to get published in top journals. Siân Evans was on one of my Writing Up Your Research for Publication workshops and it worked for her.

(2)   Like cheese, research 'goes off' if you do not package it and get your paper off to a journal editor (cheese buyer) as soon as you can.

Other points made in the article neatly summarise those to be found in this book.

A workshop that has changed my practice
Selling cheeses – a beginner's guide

'Think of yourselves as cheese makers,' said the tutor. Just as cheese makers must bring their cheese to the attention of the public via cheese sellers, so you must package your research to appeal to the cheese sellers (otherwise known as journal editors) and the cheese buying public (journal readers). Being in public health, this was perhaps an unfortunate analogy given recent scares concerning *E coli* and *Listeria*. However, it did serve to demystify what can at times appear to be a distant goal, attainable to only a select few.

    Rule one: If left in a drawer for several months research (just like cheese) will go off. Several tutees, myself included, shift uncomfortably in their seats. 'Getting more publications' was identified as a training priority at my annual appraisal (as it had been the previous year and the year before that). Thus, the workshop Writing Up Your Research for Publication seemed to offer just what the appraisal panel ordered.

    Rule two: First know your journal. There's little point in sending marscapone to a journal that handles only cheddar. Identify the top journals suitable for your product (the science citation reports are useful in assessing the impact factor of any journal) and get to know their content and style.[1] Read the instructions for authors and package your cheese appropriately.

Rule three: Always remember that editors need you. A series of rejection letters makes this a little difficult to accept but where would journals be without authors?

Rule four: Believe in your work and aim high. Don't rule out top quality journals because you believe your work is not good enough. You may be pleasantly surprised.

Rule five: If at first you don't succeed. … If your paper is rejected by your first choice journal it is not the end of the world and doesn't (necessarily) mean that your work is flawed. Was the paper appropriate for the journal selected? Had the journal recently published a series of papers on similar topics? Remember that referees are not infallible and will frequently disagree. It is okay to challenge referees' comments if they are clearly wrong. Don't give up. Repackage your work and resubmit to the next journal on your publishing list.

Rule six: Once your paper is accepted…. . Remember editors and publishers work to tight deadlines. Check proofs using standard proof correction marks (to be found in *The Writer's Handbook* or available from British Standards Institute) and return to the editor promptly.[2]

The workshop provided an insight into the publishing world and made the chances of getting research published seem possible (if not necessarily easy). In future when I am struck by writer's block, I will turn to mind mapping to get my thoughts on paper.[3] I will always aim high when selecting journals for publication (the BMJ is not out of reach) and will not let rejection get me down (too much).

With thanks and apologies to Dr Philip Hills, Centre for Research into Human Communication and Learning, Cambridge.

Siân A Evans, *senior registrar in public health medicine, Leeds*

1   Institute for Scientific Information. *Journal citation reports on CD-ROM 1995. Computer file: science edition*. Philadelphia: Institute for Scientific Information, 1996.
2   Turner B. *The writer's Handbook*. London: MacMillan, 1998.
3   Buzan T. *The mind mapping book*. London: BBC Publications, 1994.

Index